A Look At Cash Compensation for Active-Duty Military Personnel

Beth J. Asch

James R. Hosek

Craig W. Martin

Prepared for the
Office of the Secretary of Defense

RAND

National Defense Research Institute

The research described in this report was sponsored by the Office of the Secretary of Defense (OSD). The research was conducted in RAND's National Defense Research Institute, a federally funded research and development center supported by the OSD, the Joint Staff, the unified commands, and the defense agencies under Contract DASW01-01-C-0004.

Library of Congress Cataloging-in-Publication Data

Asch, Beth J., 1958–
    A look at cash compensation for active-duty military personnel / Beth J. Asch, James R.
Hosek, Craig W. Martin.
        p. cm.
    "MR-1492."
    Includes bibliographical references.
    ISBN 0-8330-3174-0
    1. United States—Armed Forces—Pay, allowances, etc. I. Hosek, James R. II. Martin,
Craig W. III.Title.

UC74 .A8335 2002
355.6'4—dc21

                                                                                            2002021395

Published 2002 by RAND
1700 Main Street, P.O. Box 2138, Santa Monica, CA 90407-2138
1200 South Hayes Street, Arlington, VA 22202-5050
201 North Craig Street, Suite 202, Pittsburgh, PA 15213-1516
RAND URL: http://www.rand.org/
To order RAND documents or to obtain additional information, contact Distribution
Services: Telephone: (310) 451-7002; Fax: (310) 451-6915; Email: order@rand.org

PREFACE

This report presents an overview of military compensation for active-duty officer and enlisted personnel in 1999. It provides information on the receipt and amount of each type of cash pay, highlighting the patterns by year of service, occupational area, and branch of service. It also quantifies the range of variation in military pay and includes data on private-sector pay variation for comparison. The report should be of interest to policymakers and to researchers concerned with military compensation

The research was undertaken for the ninth Quadrennial Review of Military Compensation, whose purpose is to investigate the adequacy of the military compensation system and recommend improvements as needed. The Office of Special Projects and Research, Office of the Under Secretary of Defense for Personnel and Readiness, sponsored the research. The research was conducted in the Forces and Resources Policy Center at RAND's National Defense Research Institute, a federally funded research and development center sponsored by the Office of the Secretary of Defense, the Joint Staff, the unified commands, and the defense agencies.

CONTENTS

FIGURES

Every four years, the Quadrennial Review of Military Compensation (QRMC) examines the level and structure of military compensation to ensure that it continues to enable the armed services to meet its manpower requirements in a timely and cost-effective manner. An area of interest to the ninth QRMC is the degree to which military pay varies among personnel and the extent to which special and incentive (S&I) pays contribute to total military pay. These pays are the key tool the services have to manage personnel flexibly and to vary pay in response to internal and external factors, such as the civilian economy, that affect their ability to attract and retain personnel.

Because military compensation consists of a large array of pays and allowances, it is unclear the degree to which total cash compensation differs among military personnel. All military personnel receive basic pay. Basic pay is based on a pay table common to all personnel, regardless of occupation and branch of service. The services also make extensive use of the various S&I pays. In addition to providing the services with the flexibility to vary pay among personnel, these pays also enable them to recognize unusual duties and hazards and to provide individuals an incentive to enlist or reenlist in hard-to-fill skill areas. The common pay table, and the relative importance of basic pay in total cash compensation, would argue for substantial similarity in pay among military personnel. But the diversity and differential use of S&I pays by the services would argue for substantial pay differences among servicemembers and a substantial role for S&I pays.

The purpose of this report is to investigate the role of the different components of military pay in total cash compensation, with attention paid to the role of S&I pays. We examine how large a portion of compensation consists of S&I pays and how much of the variance in compensation stems from S&I pays. We also consider how cash compensation varies among officer and enlisted personnel, by service, occupational group, and years of service. Since the competitiveness of military pay depends on how it compares to civilian pay opportunities, we also compare the variation in military cash compensation to the range in civilian earnings.

This report focuses on describing military compensation and not on the important behavioral outcomes that result from variations in military pay. Our analysis is related to another study conducted by Kilburn, Louie, and Goldman (2001) that also examines the role of different pay components in determining the level and variance of enlisted military compensation. Our analysis builds on this study by considering officers, not just enlisted personnel, by examining differences among occupational groups, and by using more data for a more recent year, 1999, as described below.

DATA AND ANALYTICAL APPROACH

Our analysis considers average values of military cash compensation and the average values of different components of cash compensation for active-duty officer and enlisted personnel in a single year, 1999. As described above, we examine differences in the average values by service branch, by occupational groups, and by years of service. We also examine the variance in compensation by considering both the standard deviation in pay and the difference between the 90th and 10th percentile of military compensation by service branch and years of service.

The analysis relies on three sources of data. The first is the Joint Uniform Military Pay System (JUMPS) files for each of the 12 months of calendar year 1999, provided by the Defense Manpower Data Center (DMDC). These data indicate the incidence and actual dollar amounts of each pay component received by each servicemember in each month.

The second source, also provided by DMDC, is known as the Proxy Personnel Tempo (PERSTEMPO) data file, a data set that provides monthly information on the characteristics of active-duty personnel, including occupation, service, and date of entry into the military. PERSTEMPO records for nine months of 1999 were matched to the pay records for 1999. For characteristics in the PERSTEMPO data that vary with time, such as years of service, we used the value of the characteristic as of September 1999—i.e., the end of FY 1999. Because the inflow and outflow of personnel during a year can affect the computation of annual pay, we restricted the analysis to members who served all 12 months of 1999. A final data restriction is that our analysis of officers was limited to officers whose commissioning source was either a military academy or ROTC. We exclude those who were direct appointments or who were commissioned through Officer Candidate School (OCS) or Officer Candidate Training (OCT) because these individuals tend to have high pay grades for their years of service (in the case of direct appointments) or have low officer pay grades for their years of service (in the case of OCS). Including these individuals might result in misleading figures about how the average value of officer pay varied by years of service.

The third source is information provided by the Directorate of Compensation in the Office of the Secretary of Defense (OSD) on the average amount of BAH (basic allowance for housing), BAS (basic allowance for subsistence), and the federal tax advantage for 1999 by pay grade, year of service, and marital status. These averages were merged with the PERSTEMPO and JUMPS data. We used these averages rather than the actual values of these variables provided in the JUMPS data to place all personnel on an equal footing. Because members living in military housing receive zero benefits, using the actual dollar values would assign a zero value to their housing and, therefore, would bias our estimate of the housing benefit downward.

For the purposes of our analysis, we define total cash compensation to include BAS, BAH, S&I pays, bonuses, and the federal tax advantage that arises because some allowances are not subject to federal income tax. In short, cash compensation represents the pays that would appear in a member's monthly paycheck. While health benefits, future retirement benefits, and other forms of compensation are also important factors affecting manpower supply, they are not included in our definition of cash pay. The traditional definition of cash pay is Regular Military Compensation (RMC), which is the sum of basic pay, BAH, BAS, and the tax advantage. Our definition of total cash pay expands on the traditional definition because in addition to the components that constitute RMC, we also examine other miscellaneous allowances, S&I pays, and bonuses. Thus, we can analyze the role S&I pays play in total cash compensation.

RESULTS

The main result of our analysis is that considerable variation exists among the services in the incidence and average amounts of non-RMC pays and allowances. Nonetheless, these differences are overshadowed by the similarity in the average amount of RMC. The similar values of RMC at a given year of service and the fact that RMC accounts for 85 percent or more of average total cash compensation means that average cash compensation is quite similar across military personnel at a given year of service, regardless of branch of service or occupational group. Some exceptions can be found among certain officer communities, specifically doctors, aviators, and nuclear officers. Officers in these skill areas receive S&I pays that are quite large and that increase their pay well above the average pay in other skill areas.

As Table S.1 shows, average annual cash compensation in 1999 for officers varied from $62,161 in the Marine Corps to $66,883 in the Air Force. For enlisted personnel, it varied from $29,355 in the Marine Corps to $33,744 in the Navy. By far, most of cash compensation is explained by the traditional measure of cash pay—namely RMC. In the case of officers, RMC varied from $58,707 for the Marine Corps to $61,689 in the Army. Most of the variation across service branches in average annual cash pay and in RMC stems from differences in the years of service and pay grade distributions across the services. Because basic pay in the pay table varies by years of service and pay grade, differences in the distributions can result in variations in pay across services. Still, even when we conduct the analysis by year of service, we find remarkable similarity in average annual pay across the services at a given year of service.

The dollar amounts of S&I pays, bonuses, and miscellaneous allowances and cost-of-living allowance (COLA) shown in Table S.1 are unconditional averages—i.e., they are computed across everyone in a particular branch of service. As Table S.1 shows, the average amounts of S&I pays and, therefore, the portion of average annual pay attributable to these pays are quite small. This result partly arises from the relatively low incidence of some pays and/or partly from the relative small dollar value of the pays among those who receive it.

Table S.1

Average Amounts of Cash Compensation, 1999 (Dollars)

	Army	Air Force	Marine Corps	Navy
Officers				
RMC	61,689	61,599	58,707	59,761
S&I pays	927	2,810	1,889	3,134
Miscellaneous Allowances/COLAs	837	779	810	872
Bonuses	673	1,695	756	2,172
Annual Pay	64,125	66,883	62,161	65,940
Enlisted Personnel				
RMC	30,509	31,398	28,241	30,655
S&I pays	482	301	317	1,345
Miscellaneous Allowances/COLAs	832	1,015	785	967
Bonuses	372	381	11	777
Annual Pay	32,195	33,095	29,355	33,744

We examined the incidence of different pays and the average dollar amounts among those who receive them. The incidence of different S&I pays varies across the services and across the pay types. In most cases, even when the pay is relatively common throughout the enlisted or officer force, the average dollar amount among those who receive it tends to be small. For example, among enlisted personnel, between 12 and 26 percent of personnel received hostile fire pay in 1999, depending on service. Still, the average dollar amount of hostile fire pay among those who received it was only between $433 and $633. An exception to this finding is officer Aviation Career Incentive Pay. This pay is relatively pervasive, particularly in the Air Force, Marine Corps, and Navy (between 33 and 42 percent for those three services) and the average dollar figure was relatively high, between $5,456 and $6,155.

In a few cases, the incidence of a pay is quite small, but the average dollar amount is high for those who receive the pay. For example, less than 1 percent of Army officers receive the medical officer retention bonus, but the average bonus is $36,260. Similarly, only 7.6 percent of Air Force officers receive the Aviation Officer Continuation Bonus, but the average dollar amount is $17,657. Not surprisingly, S&I pays are an important portion of total cash compensation for individuals in these specific skill areas.

Among the enlisted force, one of the more important sources of pay is enlistment and reenlistment bonuses. The incidence of enlistment bonuses was the highest in the Army, and yet, in 1999, only 3 percent of Army enlisted members received enlistment bonuses. The incidence of reenlistment bonuses was the highest in the Navy, and about 15.5 percent received a reenlistment bonus in that service. These percentage figures include both initial payments of bonuses and anniversary payments.

The incidence of bonuses varies by years of service, as would be expected, given that bonuses are targeted to personnel making enlistment or reenlistment decisions in early and midcareer. For example, between YOS 5 and 11, upward of 40 percent of Navy enlisted personnel receive a reenlistment bonus, far higher than the 15.5 percent figure computed across individuals at all YOS. Nonetheless, as mentioned earlier, RMC represents such a large fraction of average total cash compensation, that even when we consider the role of bonuses in total compensation by year of service, we still find that bonuses play a relatively small overall role during YOS 5–11.

We also consider the size and determinants of the variation in military pay and how its variation compares to the variation in civilian earnings. We examine the range of cash compensation by considering the difference between the highest and lowest deciles (i.e., the 90th and 10th percentiles) of pay at each year of service. To examine the determinants of the variation, we compute the standard deviation of four increasingly inclusive measures of pay, RMC, RMC plus S&I pays, RMC plus S&I pays plus bonuses, and RMC plus S&I pays plus bonuses plus miscellaneous allowances and COLAs.

The difference between the highest and lowest deciles varies somewhat by year of service. For enlisted personnel, the difference is about $8,000 at YOS 5, about $10,000 at YOS 10, about $12,000 at YOS 20, and about $11,000 at YOS 25. Thus, the largest difference is in midcareer, although it does not change much after YOS 10. In part, the range of variation at each YOS reflects differences in pay grade. Bonuses and S&I pays add to the variation.

We compared the difference between the 90th and 10th percentile of military average cash pay by year of service with the difference between the 90th and 30th percentile of civilian average earnings, computed from the Current Population Survey by Professor John Warner at Clemson University. The computation was limited to males with some college education and was made for each year of experience to allow comparison with military pay. We used the 30th percentile as the lower bound because civilians who do not score well on the Armed Forces Qualification Test (AFQT) or who are not high school diploma graduates are unlikely to qualify for enlistment into the military but are likely to be found among those in the lowest percentiles of the civilian earnings distribution.

The key conclusion of our military and civilian comparison is that the variation in civilian pay as measured by the difference between the 90th and 30th percentile is far larger than the range in enlisted earnings. For example, at 10 years of experience, the difference in civilian earnings is about $23,000, far higher than the $10,000 difference found between the 90th and 10th percentile of military pay at YOS 10. At 20 years of experience, the civilian difference was about $30,000, again far higher than the $12,000 figure we found for enlisted personnel. It is important to note that the civilian earnings figures are averaged across many civilian firms that differ in hiring requirements, occupational mixes, industry conditions, and location-specific conditions. Although the military's workforce is diverse, it is far more homogeneous in terms of these factors than the civilian economy at large is. Nonetheless, the range of variation among civilian males with some college is far larger than the range for enlisted personnel, more than we might expect because of the heterogeneity of the civilian labor market.

To understand the extent to which the components of military pay contribute to variation in military cash pay, we examined the standard deviation of pay for the four, increasingly inclusive, measures of pay given above. Because some of the pay components, notably BAH, BAS, and the tax advantage, are averages from OSD, their contribution to the variance of total pay will be understated. The result is that the variance in RMC (which is the sum of basic pay, BAS, BAH, and the tax advantage) at a given year of service will reflect differences in pay grade and marital status of personnel at a given year of service.

The findings regarding the determinants of variance differ across the services. For the Air Force, the standard deviation of enlisted pay is in the $3,000 to $4,000 range over most years of service, with about half due to bonuses during YOS 4 to 11, after which variation in RMC accounts for most of the difference. The variation stemming from RMC reflects the diversity of pay grades in those years of service for the Air Force. Notably, S&I pay components (excluding bonuses) account for little of the variation in Air Force pay. For the Army, the standard deviation of enlisted pay lies within a fairly narrow band between $3,000 and $4,000 during YOS 6–25 and even less in YOS 1–5. Unlike the Air Force, pay variation stemming from RMC is more prominent in the early career (YOS 1–8) because of the greater diversity of pay grades in the Army in those years of service. The variation due to S&I pays are also greater than in the Air Force.

For the Marine Corps, the variation in enlisted pay rises steadily from about $1,500 at YOS 1 to $5,000 at YOS 24. The increase is due to variation in RMC and miscellaneous allowances and COLAs. The Marine Corps makes little use of bonuses. The Navy has the greatest variation in enlisted pay among the services. Between YOS 1 and 4, the standard deviation of pay rises from $2,000 to $5,000, with most of the increase arising from bonuses. Over the YOS 5 to YOS 25 period, the standard deviation is in the $5,000 to $6,000 range, with much of the variation coming from bonuses and much coming from S&I pays, especially sea pay. As in the Air Force, bonuses play a prominent role in the Navy in creating pay differentials during early and mid-career for enlisted personnel.

Among officers, the standard deviation of RMC for the Air Force, Army, and Navy is nearly $8,000 in the first few years of commissioned service, then declines to less than $4,000 in YOS 4–12. The Marine Corps figures are a bit higher. S&I pays add about $1,000 to the standard deviation, and bonuses add substantially to pay variance. However, it is important to recall that bonuses are generally received by only a small percentage of officers, although as noted earlier, some bonuses amounts are quite substantial, especially the amounts given to doctors, aviators, and those in the nuclear fields.

CONCLUSIONS

The main conclusion stemming from our analysis is the high degree of similarity in cash compensation among military personnel at each year of service, regardless of branch of service or occupational group. In other words, although pay grows over a military career, pay is remarkably similar among personnel at the same year of service. A few notable exceptions exist, such as officers in the medical, aviation, and nuclear fields who receive S&I pays and bonuses that substantially increase their average compensation. Apart from these exceptions, equity in compensation seems to prevail. Thus, despite the large number of S&I pays, they play a relatively small role in determining average total cash compensation.

The small role of non-RMC components of pay in determining average total cash compensation is explained in part by the relatively small fraction of personnel who receive the non-RMC components of pay—i.e., S&I pays, bonuses, and miscellaneous allowances and COLAs. Even in cases where the incidence of these pays is fairly pervasive, such as the Clothing and Uniform allowance, their average dollar values tend to be small. For example, nearly all personnel receive the clothing allowance, but the average amount is less than $400 for enlisted personnel and less than $600 for officers. The similarity in pay outcomes and relatively small overall role of non-RMC components also stem from the common foundation of basic pay and similarities in the services' promotion systems in terms of promotion phase points and promotion criteria.

These similarities in compensation across personnel and the similarities in the promotion systems provide tangible evidence of the military's commitment to equity of pay opportunities—regardless of skill area. Nonetheless, that equity results in remarkable similarity in the retention profiles of personnel across the services and across occupational groups. In other words, the experience mix of occupational groups varies relatively little within each service, despite the enormous diversity in the skill requirements and duties of the personnel in these groups. Further, although notable differences exist in the experience mix across the services, with the Marine Corps having a more junior force and the Air Force having a more senior force, the similarities in the experience mixes of personnel in the different services are also notable. To the extent that the services would like to achieve more variable career lengths and more diversity in the experience mix of different occupations, the analysis in this report suggests that greater differentiation in military pay and changes in the structure of military compensation may be required.

ACKNOWLEDGMENTS

This research would not have been possible without the compensation and personnel files supplied by the Defense Manpower Data Center, the major repository of data on military personnel and compensation. We are also deeply grateful to Curtis Gilroy and John Enns, director and co-director of the ninth Quadrennial Review of Military Compensation, for their guidance, support, and commitment to this work. We appreciate comments received on earlier versions of this research from members of the QRMC Working Group, as well as from our colleagues at RAND. John Warner kindly provided predicted percentiles of private-sector earnings. Susan Everingham, director of RAND's Forces and Resources Center, provided thoughtful observations on many aspects of our QRMC work and helped delineate connections between this and other personnel projects within the center. We are grateful to our reviewers, Charles Goldman at RAND and Glenn Gotz at the Institute for Defense Analyses.

ACIP	Aviation Career Incentive Pay
AFQT	Armed Forces Qualification Test
BAH	Basic Allowance for Housing
BAS	Basic Allowance for Subsistence
COLA	Cost-of-living allowance
CONUS	Continental United States
DMDC	Defense Manpower Data Center
FSA	Family Separation Allowance
IT	Information technology
JUMPS	Joint Uniform Military Pay System
MWR	Morale, welfare, and recreation
OCS/OCT	Officer Candidate School/Officer Candidate Training
OSD	Office of the Secretary of Defense
PERSTEMPO	Personnel tempo
QRMC	Quadrennial Review of Military Compensation
RMC	Regular Military Compensation
ROTC	Reserve Officer Training Corps
S&I	Special and incentive (pays)
SRB	Selective Reenlistment Bonus
YOS	Year of Service

Chapter One

INTRODUCTION

Every four years, the level and structure of military compensation are reviewed to determine their adequacy for meeting the military personnel supply needs of the services. Military compensation presents a complicated picture because of the large number of special and incentive (S&I) pays and allowances that have been created over time. These pays and allowances address specific concerns about such factors as housing costs, dangerous duty, arduous duty, separation from family, and pay differences related to particular skill areas, such as medicine and aviation. It is possible that they create wide differences in military compensation among personnel.

At the same time, military compensation is built on the foundation of basic pay. The Army, Navy, Air Force, Marine Corps, and Coast Guard share the same basic pay tables for officers and enlisted personnel. These common basic pay tables may lead to the expectation that the actual level of military compensation by year of service and pay grade (rank) is similar across the services.

Further, if basic pay were the dominant element of military compensation, the fact that basic pay tables are common across the services implies that servicemembers face largely similar compensation incentives to remain in service. If so, one might expect a high degree of similarity in retention profiles by year of service, across the services. However, the services differ in their desired personnel force structure—for example, the Marine Corps prefers a heavily junior force. Its first-term reenlistment rate is about half that of the other services. Thus, compensation incentives are not the only mediator of the personnel force structure. Even so, common basic pay tables and similar promotion practices would suggest a small amount of pay diversity among retained personnel, which is the opposite of what one might expect from the many S&I pays and allowances.

The purpose of this report is to put S&I pays in perspective as elements of military cash compensation. We investigate how large a portion of military compensation they currently represent and how much they contribute to the variance in military compensation across personnel. Although military compensation is a pivotal factor in determining recruiting and retention outcomes, this report is intended to describe military compensation rather than relate it to behavioral outcomes.

Given the recruiting difficulties experienced in the late 1990s by the Army, the Navy, and the Air Force and the retention problems experienced in some occupational areas, it is of interest to consider how military compensation differs among subgroups and how it compares to civilian pay. Furthermore, the dispersion of earnings in the private-sector economy has grown since the early 1980s, and differences in skill, education, and ability help explain that trend. Given the importance of private-sector earnings opportunities relative to military earnings opportunities in the retention decision, it is also of interest to understand the amount of variation in military earnings and the importance of skill versus other factors (such as location or duty type) in explaining that variation.

A recent RAND study (Kilburn, Louie, and Goldman, 2001) examined patterns in the level and variance of enlisted compensation among some subgroups, but the study did not examine components of compensation among other subgroups, most notably in different occupational areas or among officers. This report provides information to fill that gap. We address the following questions:

- What is the relative size of different components of pay over enlisted and officer careers? The components include basic pay, allowances, S&I pays, bonuses, and the federal tax advantage.

- How do enlisted and officer pay profiles vary by service and by occupational area?

- How do the level and range of variation in military pay compare to the level and range in civilian pay?

Chapter Two defines the elements of military compensation addressed in this report and describes the sources of data. Chapter Three presents a variety of pay comparisons in tables and figures, and Chapter Four contains our conclusions.

PAY DEFINITION AND DATA

DEFINITION OF MILITARY PAY

We focus on the cash elements of military compensation for active-duty personnel. These include basic pay, Basic Allowance for Subsistence (BAS), Basic Allowance for Housing (BAH), S&I pays, bonuses, miscellaneous allowances, and cost-of-living allowances (COLAs). The exceptions to limiting the analysis strictly to a member's cash pay are to assign BAS and BAH values to members who live in on-base housing and to include a "tax advantage" attributable to the fact that BAS and BAH are not subject to federal income tax. The allocation of BAS and BAH to members living on base assumes that BAS and BAH amounts are reasonable approximations of the value of meals and housing provided in kind. The tax adjustment puts BAS and BAH on par with other pays, all of which are pretax. Descriptions of pays and allowances may be found in the *Uniformed Services Almanac* (2001). Also, the Department of Defense is developing a military pay Web site (http://militarypay.dtic.mil).

Cash pay does not include military health care, retirement benefits, educational benefits, and the in-kind provision of training and education. It also does not include in-kind services provided through morale, welfare, and recreation (MWR) accounts such as childcare, family counseling, and recreation facilities. Kilburn, Louie, and Goldman (2001) present estimates of the value of military health care by family size, measured in terms of the private-sector health insurance premium for similar coverage. They also estimate the present discounted value of a service-member's expected retirement benefits, by year of service.

DATA

The military pay data used for this analysis cover the 1999 calendar year and indicate the incidence and level of all pays for each individual on active duty, as well as the individual's grade, occupation, year of service, and other characteristics.

We created the data file from three sources. The first is the Joint Uniform Military Pay System (JUMPS) files for each of the 12 months of calendar year 1999, provided by the Defense Manpower Data Center (DMDC). The monthly JUMPS file has a record for each active-duty member who was paid. For each type of pay, the data indicate whether the individual received the pay in that month and the dollar amount.

In this report, we present tables and tabulations based on members who were in the military for all 12 months of calendar 1999. This approach captures payments made at irregular intervals during the year and provides information about the incidence, level, and variance of pays from the perspective of career members or those contemplating a career. However, another source of pay variation comes from the turnover of military personnel during the year, and it is possible that the inclusion of members who leave the military would present a different picture of compensation. For instance, leavers might have relatively lower ranks at a given year of service or receive fewer S&I pays. Therefore, to present a perspective on pay that includes the entire population of military personnel—those who stay throughout the year as well as those who arrive or leave during the year—we prepared tabulations for a given month during the year: June. These tabulations, which appear in Appendix A, show the incidence and amount of pays in June 1999 for members present all year and for members present in June whether or not they served the entire year. Although the percentages of members receiving S&I pays and certain allowances differ somewhat in the month view versus the all-year view, the message about the relative contribution of such pays is much the same.

The second data source, also provided by DMDC, is known as the Proxy Personnel Tempo (PERSTEMPO) data file. It is built from the Active-Duty Master files and contains information on occupation and date of entry into the military. We used monthly information from the PERSTEMPO file for the first nine months of 1999; data were not available for later months. Such time-sensitive variables as occupation were taken as of September 1999. These data were then merged with the JUMPS records for each individual.

The Directorate of Compensation, Office of the Secretary of Defense (OSD), provided the final source of data. These are estimates of the average amount of BAH, BAS, and the federal tax advantage for 1999, by pay grade, year of service, and marital status for officer and enlisted personnel. We applied the average BAH, BAS, and tax advantage data to officers and enlisted, given their pay grade and marital status. This allowed us to place members on a comparable footing. If we had instead relied on actual BAH, members living in military housing would have had zero values of BAH. Also, we wanted to include the tax advantage, the OSD computation of which depends on average BAS, so we included average BAS. (The JUMPS data contain actual BAS and housing allowances at the individual level for months in which servicemembers received those allowances.)

To construct the analysis file, we merged the 12 JUMPS files for 1999, allowing us to compute total pay, by pay component, for each member. These data were merged with PERSTEMPO data to capture occupation and entry or commissioning date and OSD data on average BAH, BAS, and tax advantage by grade and marital status.

Inflow and outflow of personnel during a year can affect the computation of annual pay. Because we restricted the analysis to members who served all 12 months of

1999,[1] we excluded new entrants in calendar year 1999 except those who entered in January 1999. This restricted the number of new entrants in our data, so we included in the analysis file those who entered in October 1998 through December 1998—i.e., who entered in the first quarter of FY 1999. Thus, the "first year" members of the analysis file are an undercount of personnel in their first year but should be sufficient to provide measures of annual pay comparable with those of personnel in later years of service. Annual pay was defined as pay during the 12 months in calendar year 1999 regardless of entry date. With these restrictions and inclusions, the analysis file contained 967,000 enlisted records and 96,000 officer records, out of the 1,490,000 in the JUMPS files.

In separate tabulations of enlistment bonus incidence and amount, we included *all* personnel in the first year of service, not just those who served all twelve months of 1999. This ensured an accurate representation of the percentage of first-year personnel receiving an enlistment bonus.

The analysis of enlisted personnel includes all individuals who meet the data restrictions described in the previous paragraphs. The analysis of officers also includes individuals who meet these restrictions as well as one additional restriction. Officers must have as commissioning source either a military academy or Reserve Officer Training Corps (ROTC). We exclude individuals who were direct appointments or commissioned via Officer Candidate School (OCS) or Officer Candidate Training (OCT). The reason is that OCS/OCT officers often have more years of service as a result of entering the military as part of the enlisted force, while direct-appointment officers enter at a higher rank and so often have a higher pay grade. Because most of our pay analysis is conducted by year of service, the inclusion of OCS/OCT or direct-appointment officers would yield misleading figures about how the average value of officer pay varied by YOS. Nevertheless, we recognize that OCS, OCT, and direct appointments are significant sources of officers. Therefore, we have prepared tables (Appendix B) that include all commissioned officers and all commissioned officers and warrant officers. These more comprehensive populations are companions to the service academy/ROTC population discussed in the text. The incidence and amounts of pays are somewhat different for the more inclusive populations, but the main findings about the relative contribution of S&I pays and allowances are basically the same.

The key variables in the analysis are years of service and the different components of military pay. Years of service are measured as of September 30, 1999 (i.e., the end of FY 1999). The analysis also focuses on seven categories of pay components. The first four are basic pay, BAS, BAH, and federal tax advantage. These four constitute Regular Military Compensation (RMC). The final three categories are S&I pays, bonuses, and miscellaneous allowances. (Bonuses are often counted among S&I pays, but we treat them as a separate category.) These three categories include many different pays, as Tables 3.1 and 3.2 reveal.

---

[1]As mentioned, the tables in Appendix A allow for a comparison between an all-year population and one with an inflow and outflow of personnel.

Finally, the year-of-service numbering convention we use is as follows. "YOS 1" refers to the period *during* the first year of service. This is the usual convention. It contrasts with the convention for stating one's age, where "one-year-old" refers to an infant in the second year of life. Hence, someone who enlists for a four-year term and extends for three months would make a reenlistment decision in YOS 5.

Chapter Three

PAY LEVEL AND VARIANCE

This chapter shows that the incidence and average amounts of non-RMC pays and allowances differ across the services. These differences are overshadowed, however, by similarity in the average amount of RMC. The similar values of average RMC at a given YOS and the fact that RMC accounts for 85 percent or more of total pay mean that average total pay is similar for individuals at a given YOS, regardless of service branch or broad occupational area. That is, we find that average total pay differences at a given YOS are relatively small.

Several exceptions occur: doctors, aviators, and nuclear officers receive S&I pays and bonuses that increase their pay well above the average pay for officers in other occupational areas.

THE INCIDENCE OF PAY COMPONENTS

Table 3.1 shows the incidence and the average amount of military pay for enlisted personnel in 1999. Table 3.2 is a similar table for officers whose source of commissioning was either a military academy or ROTC. Care is needed in interpreting the enlistment bonus and Selective Reenlistment Bonus (SRB) figures because the averages in Tables 3.1 and 3.2 confound initial payment of the bonus, which may be large, with smaller anniversary payments.

Enlisted RMC (Table 3.1) averaged $30,509 in the Army, $31,398 in the Air Force, $28,241 in the Marine Corps, and $30,655 in the Navy. The Army, Air Force, and Navy averages are close to one another, suggesting an overall similarity in the services' YOS/pay grade mix. The Marine Corps, which has about 70 percent of its enlisted personnel in the first term of service, has an average about $2,000 lower.

Officer RMC (Table 3.2) exhibits virtually no difference between the Army and Air Force: $61,689 and $61,599, respectively. The Marine Corps has the lowest average at $58,707, probably reflecting the more-junior nature of its officer corps. The Navy's average, $59,761, also suggests a more-junior officer corps than that of the Army and Air Force.

As these tables make clear, the incidence and average amounts of S&I pays and of allowances varied considerably across branch of service in 1999. As expected, career sea pay is pervasive in the Navy. About 40 percent of enlisted personnel and 19 per-

Table 3.1

Incidence and Average Amounts of Enlisted Pay, 1999

Type of Pay	Army		Air Force		Marine Corps		Navy	
	Pct. Rec'g	Avg. $ Amt.	Pct. Rec'g	Avg. $ Amt.	Pct. Rec'g	Avg. $ Amt.	Pct. Rec'g	Avg. $ Amt.
Basic Pay	100.0	19,542	100.0	20,371	100.0	17,611	100.0	19,757
BAH (Green Book)	100.0	6,497	100.0	6,559	100.0	6,245	100.0	6,453
BAS (Green Book)	100.0	2,738	100.0	2,738	100.0	2,738	100.0	2,738
Tax Advantage (Green Book)	100.0	1,732	100.0	1,731	100.0	1,647	100.0	1,707
Average RMC		30,509		31,398		28,241		30,655
Foreign-Duty Pay	28.1	73	25.2	65	10.3	35	5.3	90
Proficiency Pay	6.1	2,699	3.0	2,285	5.8	2,583	9.4	2,108
Overseas Extension Pay	0.4	696	0.1	434	1.5	1,212	0.4	675
Career Sea Pay	0.1	1,314	0.0	112	9.0	205	40.5	1,624
Career Sea Pay Premium	0.0	742	0.0		0.0	734	5.1	684
Hostile Fire Pay	15.7	633	19.8	570	12.1	468	26.1	511
Diving Duty Pay	0.1	1,744	0.3	1,687	0.3	1,800	1.7	2,007
Submarine Duty Pay	0.0		0.0		0.0		7.5	2,094
Foreign Language Pay (1)	1.5	675	1.5	806	0.7	620	0.5	715
Foreign Language Pay (2)	0.2	332	0.1	360	0.0		0.0	373
Flying Pay (Crew Member)	1.0	1,688	3.1	1,979	1.3	1,847	1.9	2,120
Flying Pay (Noncrew)	0.0		0.0		0.8	1,003	0.0	
Parachute Duty Pay	10.1	1,471	0.2	1,078	0.7	1,095	0.3	1,417
Flight Deck Duty Pay	0.0	1,200	0.0	85	2.4	471	9.0	591
Demolition Duty Pay	0.4	1,567	0.4	1,641	0.3	1,475	0.5	1,406
Experiment Stress Duty	0.0	870	0.2	1,261	0.0	1,387	0.2	747
Toxic Fuels Duty Pay	0.0	261	0.3	1,507	0.0		0.0	303
Toxic Pesticides Duty	0.0	532	0.0	1,166	0.0		0.0	998
High-Altitude Low Opening	0.3	2,297	0.3	2,399	0.2	2,207	0.5	2,498
Chem Munitions Duty	0.1	927	0.0	813	0.0		0.0	546
Average S&I Pay[a]		482		301		317		1,345
FSA[b] I	1.4	181	0.7	308	0.0		0.8	180
FSA II	19.9	417	17.1	333	19.2	385	23.0	399
CONUS COLA	0.6	730	0.6	355	1.4	612	0.7	697
Overseas COLA	24.6	1,849	24.1	2,904	21.4	2,240	19.4	2,748
Clothing/Uniform Allowance	87.2	329	90.8	281	97.9	229	99.7	336
Avg Misc Allowance/ COLAs[a]		832		1,015		785		967
Enlistment Bonus	3.0	5,193	1.7	3,749	0.5	2,137	2.2	4,139
SRB	11.2	1,949	10.1	3,167	0.0		15.4	4,452
Average Bonus[a]		372		381		11		777
Average Annual Pay[a]		32,195		33,095		29,355		33,743

NOTE: Foreign Language Pay (2) is received by members who have mastered a second foreign language. FSA II is received by members who are involuntarily separated from their families.

[a]Averaged over all members, including those not receiving these pays.

[b]FSA = Family Separation Allowance.

Table 3.2

Incidence and Average Amounts of Officer Pay, Commission Source Is ROTC or a Military Academy, 1999

Type of Pay	Army		Air Force		Marine Corps		Navy	
	Pct. Rec'g	Avg. $ Amt.	Pct. Rec'g	Avg. $ Amt.	Pct. Rec'g	Avg. $ Amt.	Pct. Rec'g	Avg. $ Amt.
Basic Pay	100.0	45,322	100.0	45,127	100.0	42,675	100.0	43,558
BAH (Green Book)	100.0	10,584	100.0	10,683	100.0	10,522	100.0	10,376
BAS (Green Book)	100.0	1,887	100.0	1,887	100.0	1,887	100.0	1,887
Tax Advantage (Green Book)	100.0	3,896	100.0	3,902	100.0	3,623	100.0	3,939
Average RMC		61,689		61,599		58,707		59,761
Saved Pay	0.0		0.0		0.0		0.0	4,248
Health Professional Saved Pay	0.0		0.0		0.0		0.0	
Variable Special Pay	0.3	8,141	0.1	8,517	0.0		0.0	8,751
Board-Certified Pay	1.8	3,236	1.0	3,435	0.0		0.4	3,656
Aviation Career Incentive Pay	9.4	5,917	41.8	6,155	33.0	5,370	38.5	5,456
Responsibility Pay	0.0		0.0		0.0		0.0	
Career Sea Pay	0.0		0.0	150	0.2	418	18.9	1,272
Career Sea Pay Premium	0.0		0.0	67	0.0		3.8	544
Hostile Fire Pay	17.6	621	21.8	576	15.5	474	24.8	525
Diving Duty Pay	0.1	1,599	0.1	1,682	0.5	1,650	2.8	2,249
Submarine Duty Pay	0.0		0.0		0.0		9.9	5,004
Foreign Language Pay (1)	3.1	730	2.6	915	1.4	802	0.8	739
Foreign Language Pay (2)	0.4	349	0.1	321	0.0		0.0	400
Flying Pay (Crew Member)	0.1	1,735	0.8	1,551	0.0		0.1	1,722
Flying Pay (Noncrew Member)	0.1	1,047	0.1	604	0.1	774	0.1	728
Air Weapons Controller (Crew)	0.0	2,028	1.0	2,564	0.0		0.0	2,400
Parachute Duty Pay	11.2	1,264	0.2	1,019	1.6	1,057	0.6	1,421
Flight Deck Duty Pay	0.0		0.0		0.2	558	4.8	485
Demolition Duty Pay	0.3	1,413	0.1	1,374	0.1	547	0.8	1,360
Experimental Stress Duty Pay	0.0	1,028	0.3	1,049	0.0		0.1	785
Toxic Fuels Duty Pay	0.0		0.1	1,438	0.0		0.0	
High-Altitude Low Opening Pay	0.2	1,981	0.2	2,181	0.0	2,700	0.7	2,504
Chemical Munitions Duty Pay	0.0	964	0.0		0.0		0.0	
Average S&I Pay[a]		927		2,810		1,889		3,134
FSA I	1.3	520	0.6	603	0.0		0.7	189
FSA II	15.2	387	14.5	306	18.3	346	21.5	380
CONUS COLA	1.2	985	1.9	439	1.6	1,007	1.2	1,070
Overseas COLA	23.2	3,243	16.7	4,300	14.5	4,996	17.6	4,391
Clothing/Uniform Allowance	1.3	529	0.8	575	1.2	371	1.3	384
Personal Money Allowance	0.0	843	0.0	321	0.0		0.0	497

Table 3.2—continued

Type of Pay	Army		Air Force		Marine Corps		Navy	
	Pct. Rec'g	Avg. $ Amt.	Pct. Rec'g	Avg. $ Amt.	Pct. Rec'g	Avg. $ Amt.	Pct. Rec'g	Avg. $ Amt.
Avg Misc Allowances/ COLAs[a]		837		779		810		872
Nuclear Officer Accession Bonus	0.0		0.0		0.0		0.0	7,000
Medical Officer Retention Bonus	0.8	36,260	0.4	35,355	0.0		0.2	36,576
Nuclear Career Accession Bonus	0.0		0.0		0.0		1.2	2,039
Nuclear Career Annual Incentive Bonus	0.0		0.0		0.0		2.5	7,402
Additional Special Pay, Medical Off.	2.0	14,729	1.1	15,000	0.0	42	0.6	14,707
Incentive Special Pay, Medical Officer	0.4	20,852	0.3	18,304	0.0		0.1	22,195
Nuclear-Qualified Officer Continuation	0.0		0.0		0.0		5.5	17,435
Aviation Officer Continuation	0.0		7.6	17,657	6.8	11,136	6.7	12,163
Average Bonus[a]		673		1,695		756		2,172
Average Annual Pay[a]		64,125		66,883		62,161		65,940

NOTE: Foreign Language Pay (2) is received by members who have mastered a second foreign language. FSA II is received by members who are involuntarily separated from their families.

[a]Averaged over all members, including those not receiving these pays.

cent of officers receive career sea pay and, of these, 5 percent of enlisted personnel and 4 percent of officers also receive career sea pay premiums. Among enlisted personnel, no other S&I pay is so dominant as sea pay. Among Air Force and Army enlisted personnel, Foreign-Duty Pay covered about a quarter of individuals in 1999. Hostile Fire Pay also covered a significant fraction of personnel—about 15 percent of Army personnel, 20 percent of Air Force enlisted personnel, 12 percent of Marine Corps enlisted personnel, and 26 percent of Navy personnel. For enlisted personnel, the average of all S&I pays was $482 for the Army, $301 for the Air Force, $317 for the Marine Corps, and $1,345 for the Navy.

In a number cases, few enlisted personnel in a given service received a certain type of pay. For example, less than 2 percent of Navy personnel and less than 1 percent of personnel in the other services received Diving Duty Pay. Several instances occur where less than 1 percent of enlisted personnel in service in 1999 received a pay. Examples include Demolition Duty Pay, Experimental Stress Duty Pay, Toxic Fuels Duty Pay, and Chemical Munitions Pay.

On the other hand, even when the incidence of a pay component is relatively pervasive among servicemembers, the average dollar amount is not always large. For example, the vast majority of enlisted personnel receive a Uniform Clothing Allowance. But the average ranges from $229 to $336, a small amount compared to some of the S&I and other pays.

The incidence of different pays differs across services. In part, these differences reflect the services' pay usage choices. An important example is the SRB. As shown in Table 3.1, about 11 percent of Army, 15 percent of Navy, and about 10 percent of all Air Force enlisted personnel received an SRB payment in 1999. The program was not offered in the Marine Corps. The differences across the services also reflect differences in their occupational mix. For example, 10 percent of Army personnel received parachute duty pay, but less than 1 percent of enlisted personnel in the other services received this pay.

Among officers whose commissioning source was a service academy or ROTC, S&I pays and allowances varied across service branches as well (Table 3.2). As mentioned, S&I pays for medical officers are particularly high. For Air Force officers, Aviation Career Incentive Pay (ACIP) is among the most prevalent S&I pays, covering about 42 percent of officers commissioned from ROTC or academies.[1] This source of pay was also prevalent among Marine Corps and Navy officers. However, the average dollar amount was somewhat higher in the Air Force. The incidence and average dollar amount of Aviation Officer Continuation Pay is also higher in the Air Force, although only covering 7.6 percent of officers in 1999. Other pervasive non-RMC pay components were Hostile Fire Pay and Family Separation Pay. S&I pays in total averaged $927 for Army officers, $2,810 for Air Force officers, $1,889 for Marine Corps officers, and $3,134 for Navy officers.

ENLISTMENT AND REENLISTMENT BONUSES

Because bonus payments may be spread out over several years, the bonus figures in Table 3.1 include both those receiving a bonus for the first time and those receiving an anniversary payment. Table 3.3 contains summary information on bonus amounts distinguishing between initial and anniversary payments. In addition, Table 3.4 presents information on the percentage of personnel receiving an enlistment bonus and the average amount received, by year of service. Figures 3.1 through 3.6 present similar information for SRBs.

Table 3.3 shows that the Army used enlistment bonuses most frequently, followed by the Navy and Air Force. The Marine Corps made the least use of enlistment bonuses. Initial bonus payments average $5,249 in the Army, $4,321 in the Navy, $3,744 in the Air Force, and $2,137 in the Marine Corps. Anniversary bonus payments were less than half this size, respectively, for each service. The initial payment was large in comparison with a servicemember's basic pay: 40 percent for a soldier, 31 percent for a sailor, 29 percent for an airman, and 16 percent for a Marine.

---

[1]Table 3.2 shows that 41.8 percent of Air Force officers received ACIP, but according to the May 2001 issue of *Air Force Magazine*, the number was 23.5 percent. We have sought to reconcile these numbers. When we expanded the officer population to include all commissioned officers, the result was 32.4 percent (see Appendix B). When we removed the restriction of being present throughout 1999 and looked at officers present in September, the result was 31 percent for ROTC and academy officers and 29.5 percent for all commissioned officers. Moreover, we checked on the possibility that ACIP included Retention Bonuses in the JUMPS files. We did a frequency on the pay amounts for ACIP by month and by and large, the amounts match what is published for ACIP payments. If bonuses were given, the payment amounts would

Table 3.3

Incidence and Average Amount of Enlistment Bonus and SRB, 1999

Bonus Incidence and Amount	Army	Air Force	Marines Corps	Navy
Enlistment bonuses				
Percentage receiving first payment[a]	2.1	1.7	0.5	1.9
Average first payment	$5,249	$3,744	$2,137	$4,321
First payment as percentage of basic pay	40.1	29.2	16.5	31.3
Percentage receiving anniversary payment[a]	1.7	0.0	0.0	0.7
Average anniversary payment	$2,312	$1,200	—	$982
Anniversary payment as percentage of basic pay	17.4	9.3	—	6.6
SRB				
Percentage receiving first payment[a]	3.7	4.3	0.0	4.0
Average first payment	$3,424	$5,672	—	$8,973
First payment as percentage of basic pay	19.4	32.8	—	51.3
Percentage receiving anniversary payment[a]	7.8	6.0	0.0	14.2
Average anniversary payment	$1,060	$1,293	—	$2,388
Anniversary payment as percentage of basic pay	5.4	6.7	—	12.1

[a]Percentages are computed relative to the total number of personnel in service for all of 1999. For first-year personnel, the sample includes personnel who entered service in October–December 1998, plus those entering in January 1999, and who stayed in service throughout 1999. Because first payments of enlistment bonuses are received on entering service, but the sample contains only four-months worth of entrants (October–January), the sample undercounts the percentage of personnel receiving first payments of enlistment bonuses. Allowing for entrants throughout the year would approximately triple the percentage.

With respect to SRB use, the percentage of personnel receiving a first payment was similar for the Army, Navy, and Air Force: 3.7 percent, 4.0 percent, and 4.3 percent, respectively. However, the average amount of the first payment differed by service: Army, $3,424; Navy, $8,973; and Air Force, $5,672. The Navy first payment was equivalent to 51 percent of basic pay, on average, while the Army and Air Force bonuses were equivalent to 19 percent and 33 percent of basic pay. The Marine Corps did not use SRBs.

The percentages of personnel receiving an initial or anniversary payment shown in Table 3.3 are relative to all enlisted personnel in service throughout 1999. To obtain a precise view of bonus usage among enlistees and reenlistees, we computed bonus information by year of service. As Table 3.4 shows, the percentages of first-year personnel who received an initial enlistment bonus payment are considerably higher than the values in Table 3.3. In the Army, 8 percent of YOS 1 personnel received an initial payment, compared with 9.9 percent in the Navy, 15.5 percent in the Air Force, and 0.9 percent in the Marine Corps. The average amounts of the payments are similar to the values in Table 3.3. Table 3.4 also shows that first payments are received by

have been different. The remaining difference (29.5 minus 23.5 equals 6) may be due to different years (1999 versus 2001) or other, unknown factors.

Table 3.4

Incidence and Average Amount of Enlistment Bonuses by Year of Service, 1999

Type of Payment	Army		Air Force		Marine Corps		Navy	
	Pct. Rec'g	Avg. $ Amt.	Pct. Rec'g	Avg. $ Amt.	Pct. Rec'g	Avg. $ Amt.	Pct. Rec'g	Avg. $ Amt.
Initial payment								
YOS 1[a]	8.0	4,584	15.5	3,837	0.9	2,884	9.9	3,435
YOS 2	11.9	5,358	10.8	3,616	2.1	2,053	9.1	4,027
YOS 3	1.1	4,420	1.3	4,101	0.1	2,606	6.0	5,005
YOS 4	0.2	4,699	0.3	3,967	0.0	—	0.4	4,943
YOS 5	0.0	3,563	0.0	3,500	0.0	—	0.1	3,444
YOS 6	0.0	5,850	0.0	1,000	0.0	—	0.0	6,583
Anniversary payment								
YOS 1[a]	1.4	1,263	0.0	813	0.0	—	0.1	649
YOS 2	9.6	2,494	0.1	1,267	0.0	—	1.6	665
YOS 3	1.9	1,688	0.0	1,000	0.0	—	3.7	1,109
YOS 4	0.1	785	0.0	1,000	0.0	—	0.5	1,253
YOS 5	0.0	1,601	0.0	—	0.0	—	0.0	1,375
YOS 6	0.0	1,417	0.0	—	0.0	—	0.0	1,175

[a]The YOS 1 category includes all personnel in their first year of service in 1999, including those with less than 12 months of service during 1999. Therefore, the percentage receiving an enlistment bonus is representative of first-year personnel.

personnel in YOS 2 and higher. These higher-year payments reflect the payment of bonuses conditional on completing advanced individual training.

For SRBs, which are paid over a broader year-of-service range than enlistment bonuses, the patterns are more apparent in figures than in tables. SRBs are payable to members who have completed at least 17 months and not more than 14 years of continuous active duty. Figure 3.1 displays the percentage of Army personnel receiving a first payment or an anniversary payment of an SRB, by year of service. As shown, 8–10 percent of personnel received a first payment in the YOS 4–7 range. In YOS 5–7 more than 25 percent of Army personnel receive a bonus payment, often an anniversary payment. Therefore, over this "early midcareer" year-of-service range, bonus payments are prevalent. The percentage receiving an anniversary payment happens to peak at YOS 7, which suggests that the Army made extensive use of bonuses several years ago (i.e., offered SRBs in many specialties) and that many of the personnel who received bonuses remained in service. Figure 3.2 shows that first payments averaged $3,000–$4,000 up to YOS 7 and around $5,000 in YOS 8–13. By comparison, anniversary payments were about $1,000 up to YOS 7 and ranged around $1,500 in YOS 8–13.

Air Force SRB usage and amounts (Figures 3. 3 and 3.4) are broadly similar to the Army's. However, the Air Force appears to cover more second-term personnel with bonuses. In YOS 6–11, 20–30 percent of Air Force personnel received a bonus payment in 1999. The spike at YOS 5 (first-term reenlistment) probably indicates an intensified usage of bonuses in 1999 in response to low reenlistment rates. Also, on average the initial SRB payments are higher in the Air Force than in the Army; for YOS 4–11 initial payments are $4,000–$7,000.

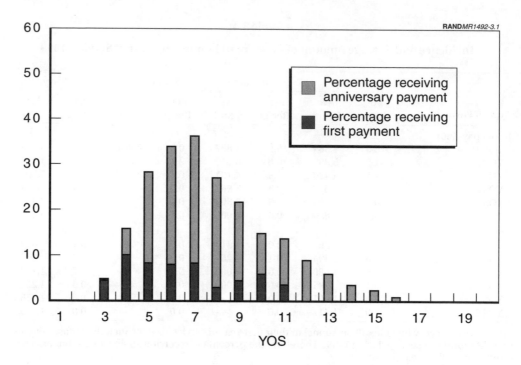

Figure 3.1—Percentage of Enlisted Personnel Receiving SRBs, Army, 1999

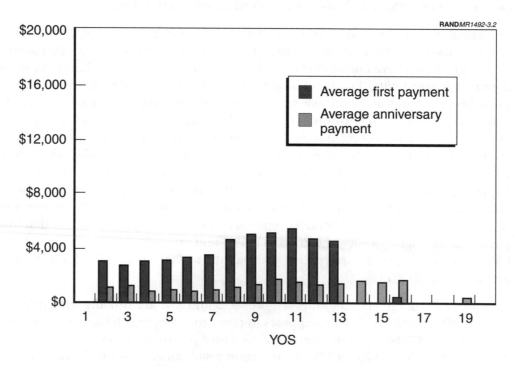

Figure 3.2—Average SRB, Army, 1999

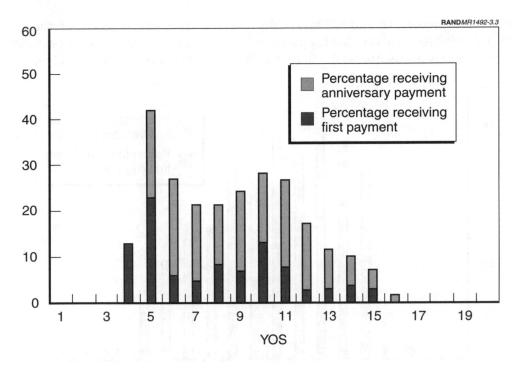

Figure 3.3—Percentage of Enlisted Personnel Receiving SRBs, Air Force, 1999

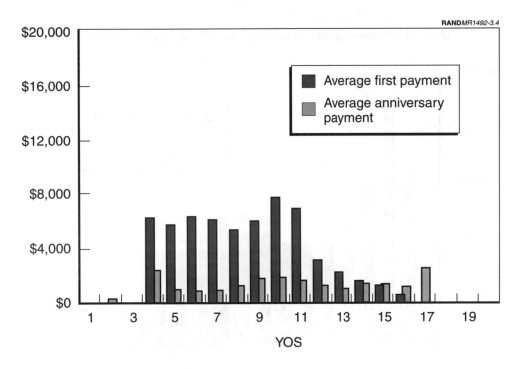

Figure 3.4—Average SRB, Air Force, 1999

The Navy (Figures 3.5 and 3.6) makes the most extensive use of SRBs and also pays higher bonuses. In YOS 5–11, upward of 40 percent of Navy enlisted personnel receive bonus payments. At first-term reenlistment, 20 percent of personnel received

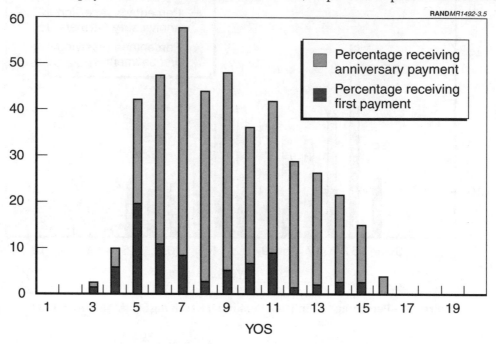

Figure 3.5—Percentage of Enlisted Personnel Receiving SRBs, Navy, 1999

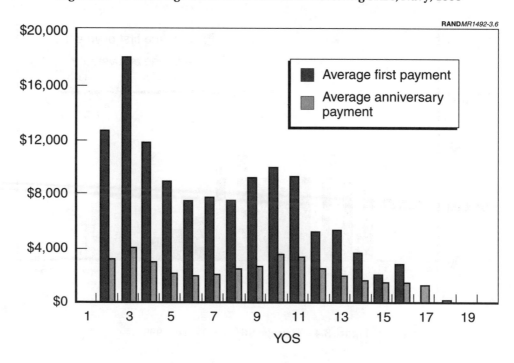

Figure 3.6—Average SRB, Navy, 1999

a bonus, and another 20 percent received an anniversary payment. In YOS 5–11, first payments averaged $7,000–$10,000, while anniversary payments were $2,000–$4,000.

AVERAGE PAY BY YEAR OF SERVICE

Despite the differences across the services in S&I and other pays and allowances shown in Tables 3.1 and 3.2, average total pay is similar across the branches of service, for a given year of service. This may be seen in Figures 3.7 and 3.8, which show average total enlisted pay and average total officer pay by service, displayed by year of service. The enlisted pay lines of the Army, Navy, and Marine Corps are quite close to one another, while the Air Force pay line is lower. The officer pay lines show a range across services that widens with year of service, reaching about $10,000 at year 20.

In the case of enlisted personnel, the lower pay line for airmen comes in part from the Air Force's longer time to E-5 promotion. This creates a relative decrement in pay that seems to persist over later years. In the case of officers, average total pay is typically higher in the Navy and the Air Force relative to the Army and then the Marine Corps. However, the Marine Corps has no doctors in its ranks, and because doctors are among the most highly paid officers their absence reduces the Marine Corps average.

When all categories of pay are included, average annual enlisted pay for a new recruit in YOS 1 is about $23,000 (Figure 3.7). Average pay has grown to about $35,000 by

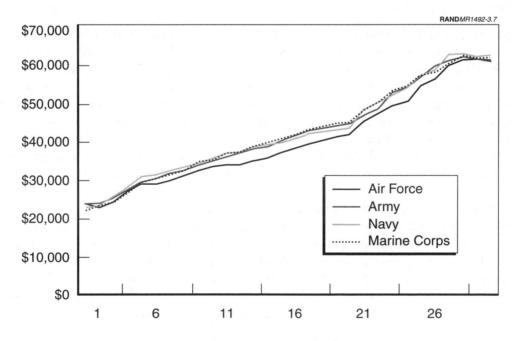

Figure 3.7—Average Total Enlisted Pay by Service and Year of Service, 1999

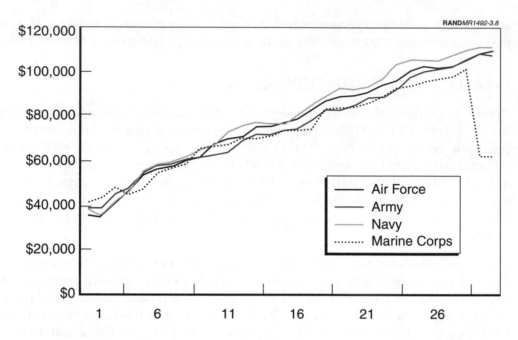

Figure 3.8—Average Total Officer Pay by Service and Year of Service, 1999

YOS 10 and $42,000 by YOS 20. Average annual pay grows steeply after YOS 20 because enlisted personnel in lower grades retire at YOS 20, and those who remain are a highly selected group of senior enlisted personnel who are in higher grades, particularly E-8 and E-9.

Although enlisted average total pay varies by year of service, it does not vary much across services for a given year of service for the Army, Navy, and Marine Corps. At YOS 10, average total pay was $35,007 for the Army, $35,675 for the Marine Corps, $35,863 for the Navy, and $33,621 for the Air Force. Again, the lower figure for the Air Force reflects a slower promotion tempo relative to the other services that tends to depress enlisted basic pay in the Air Force for a member at a given year of service. Time to E-5 is about two years slower than in the other services. It also reflects the different incidence and use of S&I pay, shown in Tables 3.1 and 3.2. Average pay also rises by year of service for officers (whose commissioning source is academy or ROTC), starting around $35,500 at YOS 1 and growing to $102,000 at YOS 30. Relative to other services, Marine Corps officers' average pay appears lower than that of Army, Navy, and Air Force officers over their careers. For example, average pay at YOS 6 was $56,000 for Air Force officers, $58,000 for Army and Navy officers, and $44,400 for Marine Corps officers. At YOS 25, average total pay was $91,262 for Air Force officers, $88,130 for Army officers, $91,202 for Navy officers, and $85,283 for Marine Corps officers. As mentioned, the Marine Corps' lower figure partially reflects the exclusion of medical officers from the Marine ranks.

Figures 3.9 and 3.10 show average enlisted pay and average officer pay separately by service and year of service and broken out by category: basic pay, BAH, BAS, federal

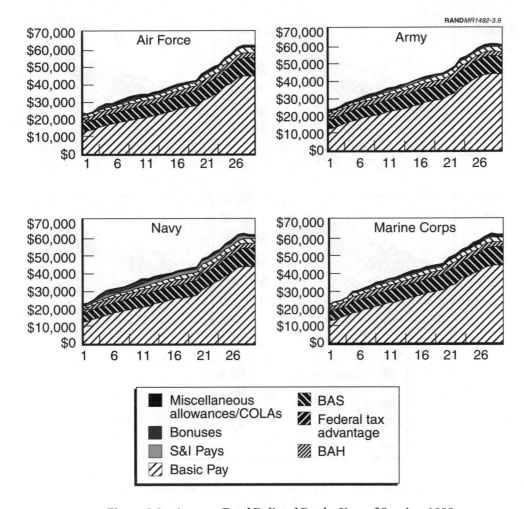

Figure 3.9—Average Total Enlisted Pay by Year of Service, 1999

tax advantage, S&I pays, bonuses, miscellaneous allowances, and COLAs. (Figure 3.10 shows the averages for officers whose source of commission was either ROTC or a military academy.) Despite the large number of pay components, most compensation comes in the form of RMC.

Figures 3.11 and 3.12 show the percentage of average pay coming from non-RMC components, by YOS, for enlisted and officers, respectively, where the non-RMC components are S&I pays, bonuses, and miscellaneous allowances. The percentage of total compensation that is not RMC is at most 15 percent and is usually less than 10 percent.

Although non-RMC components are not large on average, some identifiable variations can be found in these components by year of service and by service. That is, the services vary in their use of these components and the importance of these components differs during the course of a military career. Figures 3.9 and 3.10 make clear that the average value of non-RMC components is greatest in the early and

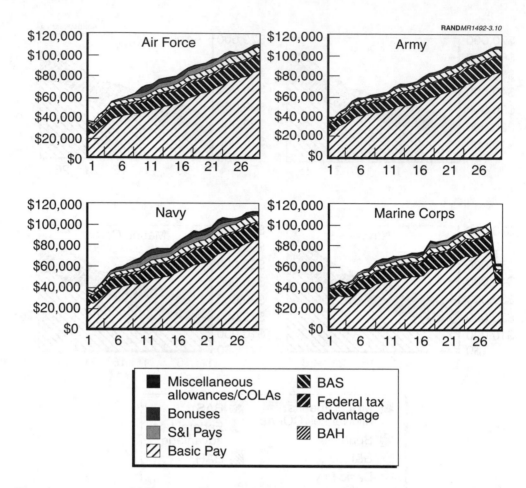

Figure 3.10—Average Officer Pay by Year of Service (Commissioning Source Is Academy or ROTC), 1999

midcareer, YOS 4–12. It is also greatest in the Navy for both officers and enlisted personnel. As shown earlier, the Navy makes significant use of bonuses, especially reenlistment bonuses and S&I pays. In part, the Navy use of these pays reflects the importance of sea pay in Navy compensation. But, even excluding sea pay, the average value of non-RMC sources of pay is largest in the Navy for enlisted personnel. In the case of officers, non-RMC components are also relatively large in the Air Force, peaking at YOS 10.

AVERAGE PAY BY OCCUPATIONAL AREA

Because of differences in the targeting of S&I pays and in promotion speed across occupational areas, we might expect average pay to vary somewhat across personnel in different areas. On the other hand, we might expect average pay to vary little by occupational area because, as shown in Figures 3.7 and 3.8, average total pay is dominated by RMC, not S&I and other pays, and the average amounts of these other pays

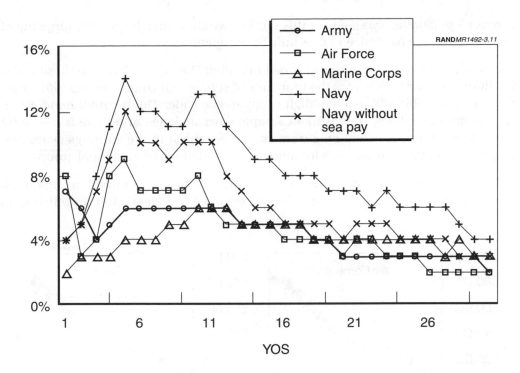

Figure 3.11—Non-RMC Components of Enlisted Pay as a Fraction of Average Total Pay, 1999

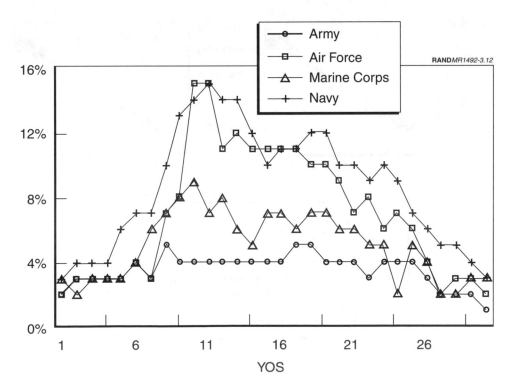

Figure 3.12—Non-RMC Components of Officer Pay as a Fraction of Average Total Pay, 1999

across all personnel are small. In this section, we show that despite the targeting of S&I pays, average pay indeed varies little by occupational area.

We define occupation in terms of broad one-digit DoD codes because these codes facilitate comparisons across the branches of service. Of course, occupations may differ considerably within a one-digit occupational code. On the other hand, when we use one-digit occupational areas, sample sizes are larger and there is less noise (i.e., variation in data stemming from smaller samples) in the earnings estimates. Later we show pay comparisons for more narrowly defined occupational groups.

Average total pay by year of service varies little by broadly defined occupational areas, as shown in Figure 3.13 for enlisted personnel and Figure 3.14 for officers. In

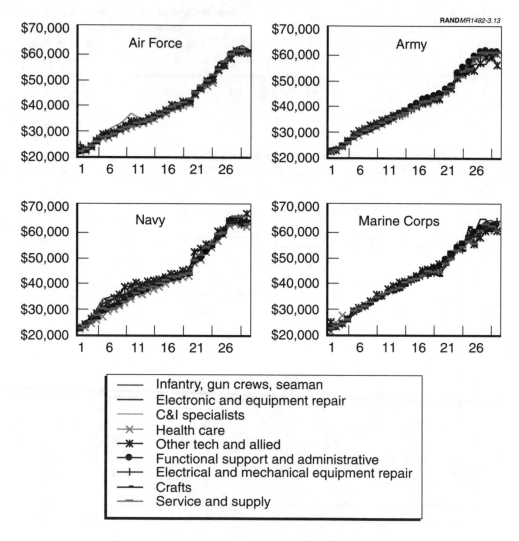

Figure 3.13—Average Enlisted Pay by Year of Service and Occupational Area, 1999

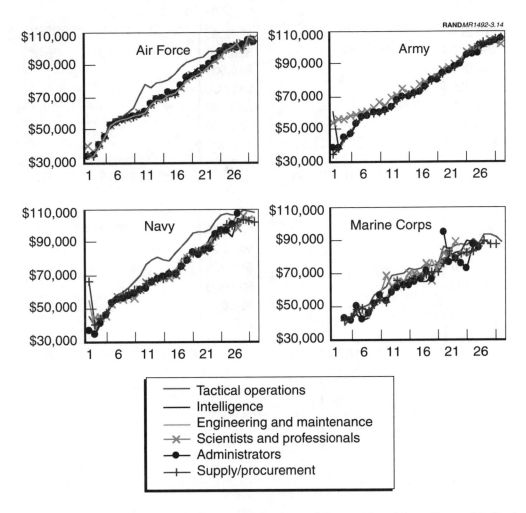

Figure 3.14—Average Officer Pay by Year of Service and Occupational Area, Except Medical Officers, 1999

part, the similarity in the average pay profiles across occupational areas reflects the broad definition of each area and each area's inclusion of many diverse occupational specialties. However, even when we define occupation more narrowly, the pay similarities remain. For example, Figure 3.15 shows the average enlisted pay profiles for information technology (IT) versus non-IT-related occupations, where IT occupations are as defined by an OSD commission on Information Technology/Information Assurance Personnel. Figure 3.16 shows the average total pay profiles for individuals in air-related versus nonair-related occupational areas, where "air"-related occupations are identified by occupational titles related to the operation, maintenance, or support of aircraft. For instance, any job title containing "pilot" or "aircraft" was determined to be air-related. Any description that indicated support or maintenance of aircraft was also included. Again, the profiles are nearly identical. Therefore, any S&I pay differences across these occupations are dominated on average by similarities in other pay components. They are also dominated by similarities in the result-

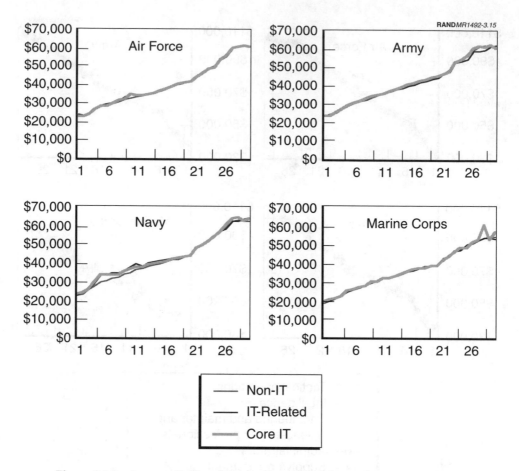

Figure 3.15—Average Enlisted Pay by Year of Service and IT-Occupational Category, 1999

ing retention and grade mix at each year of service, which influences the average pay level at each year of service in the figures.

Table 3.5 shows the FY 1999 distribution of enlisted personnel across years of service by broad occupational categories, and Table 3.6 shows the distribution for officers. The information comes from DMDC and reflects the inventory as of the end of FY 1999. Consequently, the data are not subject to the sample restrictions used to derive the figures in the earlier tables and figures.

The percentage of the force in each year of service group is quite similar across occupational areas. These figures together with the pay figures point to a clear conclusion: *in most cases, differences in pay and retention by broad occupational area are quite small.* They suggest that although S&I and other pays are used, their effect is fairly small in terms of creating much differentiation in pay. Furthermore, the similarity in the YOS mix across broad occupational areas suggests that the services provide very similar career and pay opportunities to personnel, regardless of occupational area. Still, as suggested above, exceptions to this arise: aviators, medical, and nuclear-trained personnel received comparatively large levels of special pay.

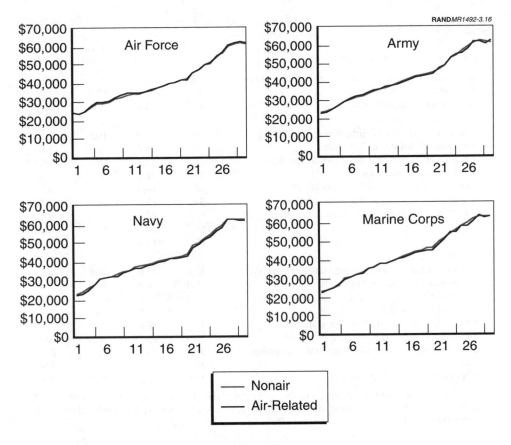

Figure 3.16—Average Enlisted Pay by Year of Service and Air versus Nonair
Occupational Areas, 1999

Table 3.5

Enlisted Year of Service Distribution by One-Digit DoD Occupational
Code, FY 1999

One-Digit Occupational Area	YOS 1–5	YOS 6–10	YOS 11–20	YOS 21–30
Army				
Infantry, Gun Crews, and Seamanship Specialists	57.3	16.9	22.6	3.2
Electronic Equipment Repairers	59.3	18.4	20.3	2.0
Communications and Intelligence Specialists	56.1	17.8	23.5	2.6
Health Care Specialists	49.3	25.0	23.1	2.6
Other Technical and Allied Specialists	48.0	20.2	28.0	3.7
Functional Support and Administration	44.6	21.9	27.7	5.8
Electrical and Mechanical Equipment Repairers	55.8	20.8	21.1	2.4
Craftsmen	61.2	19.2	17.7	2.0
Service and Supply Handlers	56.5	20.5	21.1	1.9
Navy				
Infantry, Gun Crews, and Seamanship Specialists	55.3	13.3	28.1	3.3
Electronic Equipment Repairers	39.2	20.1	37.0	3.6
Communications and Intelligence Specialists	44.6	20.8	31.5	3.2
Health Care Specialists	40.3	27.7	28.8	3.2
Other Technical and Allied Specialists	22.8	19.8	50.2	7.1
Functional Support and Administration	24.8	22.1	47.0	6.1

Table 3.5—continued

One-Digit Occupational Area	YOS 1–5	YOS 6–10	YOS 11–20	YOS 21–30
Electrical and Mechanical Equipment Repairers	46.6	18.7	31.2	3.5
Craftsmen	32.7	22.1	42.4	2.8
Service and Supply Handlers	28.2	24.5	43.6	3.7
Marine Corps				
Infantry, Gun Crews, and Seamanship Specialists	77.1	10.6	10.9	1.4
Electronic Equipment Repairers	59.9	18.6	17.7	3.7
Communications and Intelligence Specialists	59.1	17.7	19.6	3.6
Health Care Specialists	38.3	21.2	36.0	4.5
Other Technical and Allied Specialists	57.9	18.6	19.9	3.5
Functional Support and Administration	54.7	15.8	22.2	7.3
Electrical and Mechanical Equipment Repairers	63.5	17.0	16.5	3.0
Craftsmen	68.7	14.7	14.8	1.8
Service and Supply Handlers	70.2	14.2	13.2	2.3
Air Force				
Infantry, Gun Crews, and Seamanship Specialists	43.0	17.6	35.0	4.4
Electronic Equipment Repairers	33.4	18.4	41.9	6.4
Communications and Intelligence Specialists	35.9	16.8	40.8	6.5
Health Care Specialists	43.3	24.8	28.6	3.4
Other Technical and Allied Specialists	39.3	16.8	38.2	5.7
Functional Support and Administration	28.5	19.3	44.3	8.0
Electrical and Mechanical Equipment Repairers	35.5	18.4	39.4	6.7
Craftsmen	36.4	18.6	37.1	7.9
Service and Supply Handlers	36.0	22.0	35.5	6.5

NOTE: Data were obtained from DMDC and reflect the percentages in the end of FY 1999 active-duty inventory. Because the data are for a specific time, they are not subject to any sample restrictions.

Table 3.6

Officer Year of Service Distribution by One-Digit DoD Occupational Code, FY 1999

One-Digit Occupational Area	YOS 1–5	YOS 6–10	YOS 11–20	YOS 21–30
Army				
Tactical Operations Officers	31.7	22.3	34.1	11.9
Intelligence Officers	24.4	22.5	43.3	9.8
Engineering and Maintenance Officers	39.0	20.1	33.1	7.8
Scientists and Professionals	23.7	17.9	42.4	16.0
Health Care Officers	30.4	23.2	35.6	10.8
Administrators	23.1	19.5	41.0	16.5
Supply, Procurement, and Allied Officers	26.6	21.0	41.2	11.2
Navy				
Tactical Operations Officers	15.8	30.0	39.5	14.7
Intelligence Officers	20.5	22.3	43.2	14.0
Engineering and Maintenance Officers	6.7	7.1	51.1	35.1
Scientists and Professionals	17.6	23.5	43.8	15.2
Health Care Officers	29.0	22.2	36.2	12.6
Administrators	46.7	10.6	31.3	11.4
Supply, Procurement, and Allied Officers	15.2	21.2	45.5	18.1
Marine Corps				
Tactical Operations Officers	20.6	33.3	36.3	9.7
Intelligence Officers	27.1	26.5	34.4	12.0
Engineering and Maintenance Officers	16.8	20.6	37.9	24.7
Scientists and Professionals	31.1	25.5	37.0	6.3

Table 3.6—continued

One-Digit Occupational Area	YOS 1–5	YOS 6–10	YOS 11–20	YOS 21–30
Health Care Officers	32.7	22.5	36.8	8.1
Administrators	25.9	26.5	33.3	14.4
Supply, Procurement, and Allied Officers	26.7	26.7	33.3	13.3
Air Force				
Tactical Operations Officers	14.9	26.8	46.1	12.2
Intelligence Officers	28.2	23.1	33.1	15.6
Engineering and Maintenance Officers	26.9	23.1	38.9	11.1
Scientists and Professionals	25.0	21.3	39.4	14.3
Health Care Officers	30.8	22.7	36.2	10.4
Administrators	24.0	21.4	31.1	23.5
Supply, Procurement, and Allied Officers	19.4	17.4	38.6	24.5

NOTE: Data were obtained from DMDC and reflect the percentages in the end of FY 1999 active-duty inventory. Because the data are for a specific time, they are not subject to any sample restrictions.

RANGE OF VARIATION IN THE COMPONENTS OF PAY

The earlier comparisons focused on average levels of total pay. Also of interest are the size and determinants of variation in military pay and how the variation compares to variation in civilian earnings. In this section, we present information on the range of pay variation by means of plots of pay percentiles and examine the sources of variation with respect to four increasingly inclusive measures of pay. These are RMC, RMC plus S&I pays, RMC plus S&I plus bonuses, and RMC plus S&I plus bonuses plus miscellaneous allowances and COLAs. The components of these groupings match the components in Tables 3.1 and 3.2.

Figure 3.17 shows the 10th, 25th, 50th, 75th, and 90th percentiles of total pay by years of service for enlisted personnel in all services combined. Figure 3.18 shows the profiles for officers whose commissioning source was ROTC or a military academy. At the 50th percentile (or median), half of the members earned more, and half earned less, than the indicated amount. Similarly, at the 90th percentile 10 percent of the members earned more and 90 percent earned less than the indicated amount.

The difference between the highest and lowest percentile provides a measure of the variance in total pay among military personnel. The difference varies somewhat with YOS. For enlisted personnel, it is about $8,000 at YOS 5, about $10,000 at YOS 10, about $12,000 at YOS 20, and $11,000 at YOS 25. In other words, the difference is largest in the midcareer although it changes little beyond YOS 10.

The range of variation in military compensation in part reflects the different pay grades of personnel at each YOS. For instance, in the July 2000 basic pay table, the difference between an E-6 and an E-5 at YOS 10 is $2,174.10 – $1,962.90 = $211.20 per month, or $2,534.40 per year. Thus, some part of the $2,500 of the $10,000 difference at YOS 10 is due to differences in grade. Additional variation comes from differences in the receipt of S&I pays, which are related to duty (e.g., sea pay), risk (e.g., Toxic Fuels Duty Pay), skill (e.g., Foreign Language Pay), and exposure to danger during

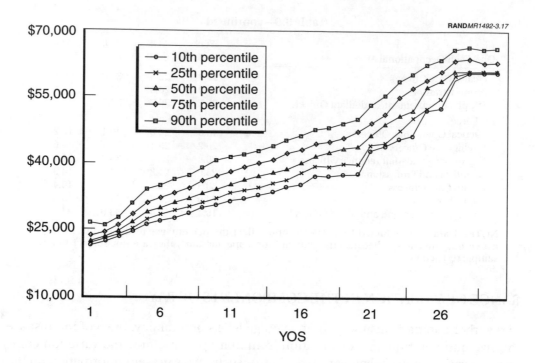

Figure 3.17—Enlisted Pay Percentiles, 1999

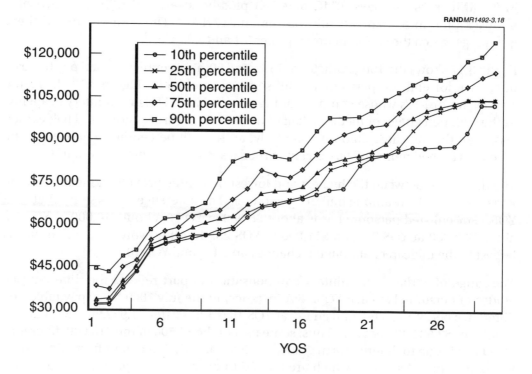

Figure 3.18—Officer Pay Percentiles, 1999

military operations (Hostile Fire Pay). Bonuses also add to the variation in pay as they vary in presence and amount across specialties and year of service. Finally, miscellaneous allowances and COLAs also vary (e.g., Family Separation Allowance, CONUS COLA, Overseas COLA).

It is interesting to compare the range of variation in enlisted earnings with the range in the civilian sector. Figure 3.19 shows the percentile of civilian earnings for males with some college in 1999.[2] We use the 30th percentile as the lower bound because the military targets high-quality enlistees who score well on the Armed Forces Qualification Test (AFQT). Such individuals are unlikely to be found in the lowest percentiles of civilian earnings, even for those with some college.

The variation in civilian pay as measured by the difference between the 90th and 30th percentiles is significantly larger than the range in enlisted earnings. For instance, at 10 years of experience, the difference is about $23,000, which may be compared with the military's $10,000 difference between the 90th and 10th percentiles at YOS 10. At 20 years of experience, the difference is about $30,000. These ranges are far larger than the ranges for enlisted personnel at similar levels of experience.

Civilian earnings figures are averaged across many civilian firms that differ in their hiring requirements, occupational mixes, industry conditions, and location-specific

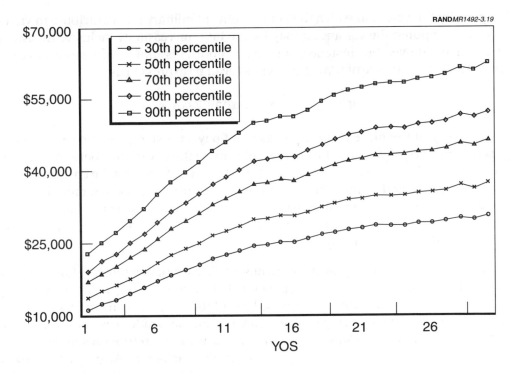

Figure 3.19—Predicted Earnings Percentiles, Civilian Males with Some College, 1999

---

[2]We thank John Warner for providing the predicted percentiles of private-sector annual earnings.

conditions. Although the military has a diverse workforce, it is more homogeneous in terms of these factors than is the civilian economy at large. For instance, the services might be thought of as a large firm with four divisions, all operating under a common basic pay table, whereas the private market contains thousands of firms, each with its own pay table. Consequently, we would expect to observe more variation in civilian earnings than in military earnings. Nonetheless, the range of variation among males with some college is far larger than the range shown in enlisted earnings—more than we might expect—because of the heterogeneity of the civilian firms.

Furthermore, by comparison with enlisted earnings, probably a minor portion of, say, the $23,000 range of variation in civilian pay at 10 years of experience is related to location or circumstance. Although speculation, it seems likely to us that much of the variation in civilian pay traces to differences in individual ability, motivation, education, and occupation. Certainly, there are geographic differences in wage, holding constant other factors. Wages tend to be lower in the South, higher in Alaska, and higher in cities, for example. Similarly, there are risk-related differences in wages. Some jobs entail a high risk of injury or impairment (e.g., police, fire fighting, construction) or a health risk (e.g., dental hygienist, mining, work involving toxic substances). Nonetheless, much of the variation in private-sector wages may stem from knowledge, skill, and ability, with knowledge and skill being the product of education, training, and experience.

To quantify the extent to which the components of military pay contribute to variation, we computed the variance of pay for the four, increasingly inclusive measures of pay given above. For instance, suppose x represents RMC and y represents S&I pays. Then the variance of RMC plus S&I pays can be expressed as

$$\mathrm{var}(x + y) = \mathrm{var}(x) + \mathrm{var}(y) + 2\,\mathrm{cov}(x, y)$$

The variance of the more inclusive measure of pay, $(x + y)$, equals the variance of x plus the variance of y, which are positive, plus twice the covariance between x and y. The variance of $(x + y)$ will be greater than the variance of x unless the covariance of x and y is negative and "large." Thus, it is possible for the variance of a more inclusive pay measure to be less than the variance of a less inclusive measure. But with rare exception, we find in our tabulations that variance increases as the pay measure includes more elements of pay.

Further, because of the way we have created RMC, its variance reflects differences in pay grade and marital status among personnel. In general, RMC includes basic pay, BAS, BAH, and the tax advantage, and the level of BAH depends on family size. However, we have used the average value of BAH given pay grade, year of service, and marital status (but not family size). RMC variance will therefore be somewhat less than its variance would be if family size were also included. Also, BAH naturally varies by locale because of differences in the cost of housing. Use of average BAH eliminates this source of variation—a source of variation that BAH is in fact intended to eliminate.

Figures 3.20 through 3.27 present the standard deviations of enlisted and officer pay, respectively, by year of service for each service, for RMC, RMC plus S&I, RMC plus S&I plus bonuses, and RMC plus S&I plus bonuses plus miscellaneous allowances and COLAs. (The standard deviation is the square root of the variance, and we use the standard deviation because its units (dollars) are comparable to those in our other tables and figures.) For Air Force enlisted (Figure 3.20), pay variation stemming from RMC is low for the first dozen years of service, rising from under $1,000 at YOS 1 to around $1,500 at YOS 12. From there, it rises rapidly to $4,000 at YOS 20. At YOS 24 it begins a rapid descent toward zero, falling below $1,000 by YOS 28. The rapid decline reflects the increasing homogeneity in rank of senior enlisted personnel—i.e., all E-8 or E-9. Similarly, the increase in variation over YOS 12–20 reflects an increasing diversity in pay grade as personnel are promoted at different speeds and reach different ranks. When S&I pays are included, little additional variation occurs; the RMC plus S&I line tracks closely the RMC line. However, the inclusion of bonuses causes a substantial increase in variation during YOS 4–11. From YOS 12 onward, bonuses contribute little to pay variation. Instead, additional pay variation comes from miscellaneous allowances and COLAs. These add about $750 to variation from YOS 12–27. As a rough gauge, the standard deviation of Air Force enlisted pay is in the $3,000–$5,000 range over most years of service, with about half due to bonuses during YOS 4–11, after which variation in RMC accounts for most of the variation.

The standard deviation of Army enlisted pay (Figure 3.21) lies within a fairly narrow band between $3,000 and $4,000 over YOS 6–25, with somewhat less variation in YOS

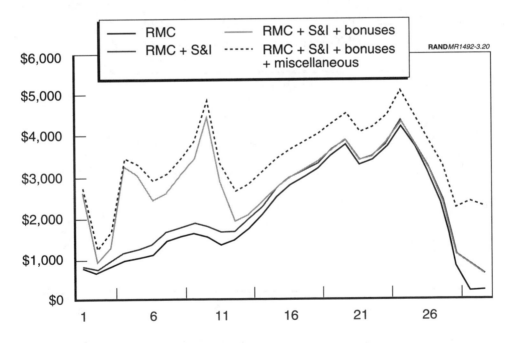

Figure 3.20—Standard Deviation of Enlisted Pay by Year of Service,
Air Force, 1999

1–5. Unlike in the Air Force, pay variation due to RMC is more prominent in YOS 1–8, while variation arising from bonuses is less prominent. This difference traces to the Air Force's slower promotion tempo; Army personnel reach E-5 about two years sooner than Air Force personnel, and at YOS 1–8 there is more diversity of rank in the Army than in the Air Force. The Army also appears to make more use of S&I pays during YOS 10–20 than does the Air Force, as variation caused by S&I pay is greater in the Army over those years.

The Marine Corps' enlisted pay variation (Figure 3.22) rises steadily from about $1,500 at YOS 1 to $5,000 at YOS 24. The increase is propelled by variation in RMC (hence variation in rank and marital status) and miscellaneous allowances and COLAs. The Marine Corps makes scant use of enlistment bonuses and does not use reenlistment bonuses, hence virtually no variation can be attributed to bonuses. (In the figure, the RMC plus S&I plus bonuses line lies directly on top of the RMC plus S&I line.)

The Navy has the greatest variation in enlisted pay (Figure 3.23). During the first term (say YOS 1–4), the standard deviation of total pay rises from about $2,000 to $5,000, with most of the increase attributable to bonuses. Further, the role of S&I pay becomes increasingly prominent over this range, probably reflecting the growing proportion of sailors who qualify for and receive sea pay. Over YOS 5–25 the standard deviation is in the $5,000–$6,000 range. Up to YOS 12, about half the variation comes from bonuses, and afterward most of the variation comes from RMC, followed by S&I pays (especially sea pay and sea pay premiums, most likely). The Navy is like

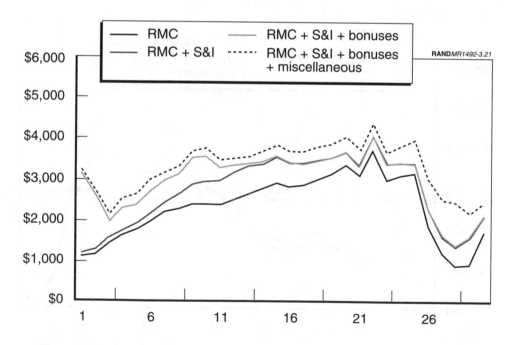

Figure 3.21—Standard Deviation of Enlisted Pay by Year of Service, Army, 1999

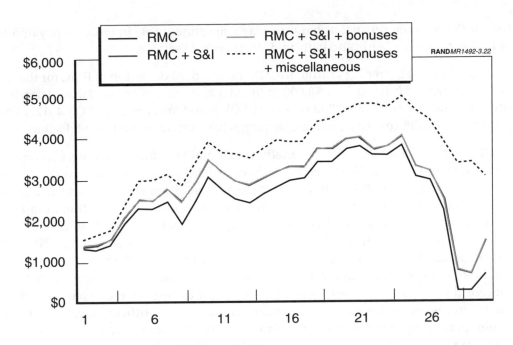

**Figure 3.22—Standard Deviation of Enlisted Pay by Year of Service,
Marine Corps, 1999**

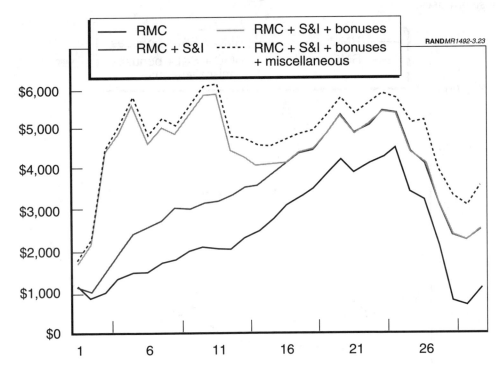

**Figure 3.23—Standard Deviation of Enlisted Pay by Year of Service,
Navy, 1999**

the Air Force in the sense that bonuses play a prominent role in creating pay differentiation during the early and early midcareer years of service.

Among officers (Figures 3.24 through 3.27), the standard deviation of RMC for the Air Force, Army, and Navy is near $8,000 in the first few years of commissioned service, then declines to around $4,000 or less at YOS 3 and still lower in YOS 4–12. The Marine Corps' figures are a bit higher although have the same pattern of decline.

In all services, the amount of pay variation attributable to miscellaneous allowances and COLAs is minimal. However, the inclusion of S&I pays adds about $1,000 to the standard deviation of RMC alone, and the further addition of bonuses adds a great deal to pay variance. The major bonuses are Aviation Officer Continuation Pay, Medical Officer Retention Bonus, Additional Special Pay for Medical Officers, Incentive Specialty Pay for Medical Officers, Nuclear Officer Accession Bonus, Nuclear Officer Retention Bonus, Nuclear Career Annual Incentive Bonus, and Nuclear-Qualified Officer Continuation Pay. Although only a small percentage of officers receive these bonuses, their large amounts significantly increase pay variation. Therefore, when examining the standard deviations of officer pay, it is worth remembering that much of the pay variation arises from bonuses received by a small proportion of officers. Around 3 percent of Army officers, 9 percent of Air Force officers, 7 percent of Marine Corps officers, and 13–14 percent of Navy officers receive these bonuses.

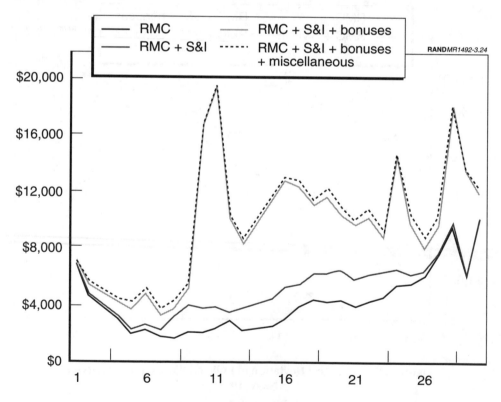

Figure 3.24—Standard Deviation of Officer Pay by Year of Service, Air Force, 1999

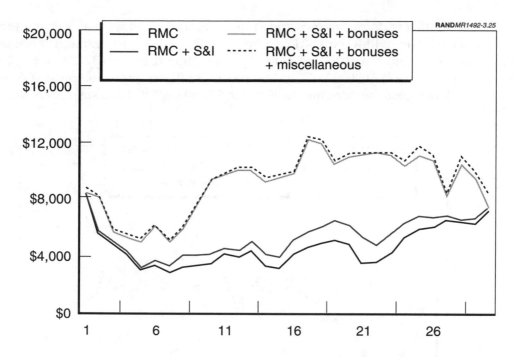

Figure 3.25—Standard Deviation of Officer Pay by Year of Service, Army, 1999

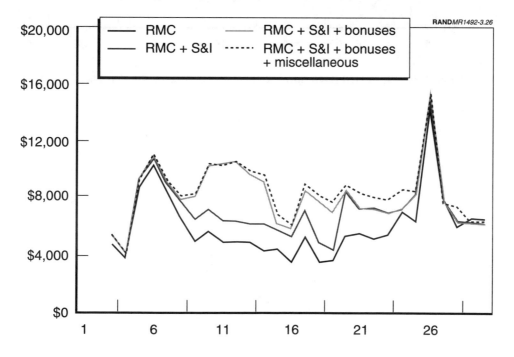

Figure 3.26—Standard Deviation of Officer Pay by Year of Service, Marine Corps, 1999

The bulk of officers do not receive any of these bonuses, and we may assume the standard deviation of RMC plus S&I pays largely reflects their pay variation. For the Air Force, Army, and Navy, this measure of pay variation rises from $2,000 to $3,000 at YOS 3 to $6,000 to $7,000 at YOS 20. Marine Corps officers' pay variation at YOS 5–7 is more than $8,000 then declines to $6,000 to $7,000 by YOS 9 and stays there until YOS 20.

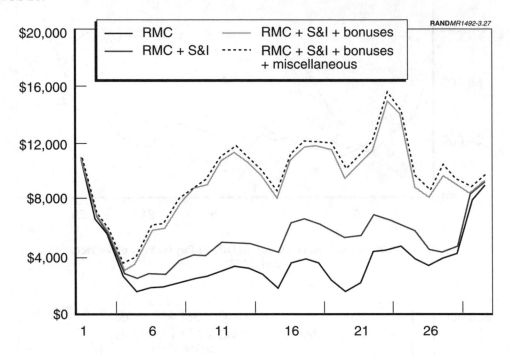

Figure 3.27—Standard Deviation of Officer Pay by Year of Service, Navy, 1999

Chapter Four

CONCLUSION

A chief finding of our research is the high degree of similarity of outcomes in military compensation across the branches of service. This is somewhat surprising in that compensation outcomes depend not only on basic pay tables, but also on service policies and servicemember decisions affecting retention and promotion. Furthermore, a host of S&I pays, bonuses, and miscellaneous allowances and COLAs lend variance to pay outcomes. Nevertheless, our findings show a striking degree of similarity in military cash compensation by year of service across the services. This is true for both officers and enlisted, with few exceptions. In particular, Air Force enlisted personnel, promoted more slowly to E-5 than personnel in other services, have slightly lower average pay by year of service. Also, officers in medical, aviation, and nuclear fields receive S&I pays and bonuses that raise their average compensation well above that of other officers. Yet apart from these exceptions, equity in compensation outcomes prevails across the services.

Although S&I pays create some variation in compensation, because these pays are typically received by few personnel and are often not large in annual amount, they do not cause prominent differences in pay. Similarly, enlistment and reenlistment bonuses result in only minor differences in average pay between bonus recipients and nonrecipients, and most personnel do not receive bonuses. Despite the fact that initial bonus payments typically represent a substantial fraction of basic pay (often on the order of one-third to two-thirds of basic pay, sometimes higher), anniversary bonus payments are lower, around $2,000. Further, miscellaneous allowances and COLAs also create fairly minor differences in compensation. For example, the Clothing and Uniform Allowance is received by nearly all personnel but is small and varies little. About one-fifth of personnel receive Family Separation Allowances, but in no case is the average annual amount greater than $500. Overseas COLAs, also received by about a fifth of personnel, average $2,000–$4,000 per year. They are a small fraction of average enlisted pay (about $32,000) and a still smaller fraction of average officer pay (about $64,000).

The similarity of cash compensation outcomes by year of service emerges from several factors. The first is a common "foundation" of pay—namely RMC. In addition, the services have similar promotion criteria and promotion phase points, although we grant that each service has its own criteria and promotion system. (The services' enlisted promotion criteria are described in Williamson [1999].) Finally, as mentioned, S&I pays, bonuses, and miscellaneous allowances and COLAs do not average out to large amounts. RMC accounts for $30,000 of the $32,000 average enlisted pay and $60,000 of the $64,000 average officer pay (Tables 3.1 and 3.2).

Given the common foundation of pay, similar promotion systems, and relatively small average amounts of non-RMC pays, it is not surprising to find highly similar patterns of retention. Retention profiles are most alike across occupational areas within a service. Of course, reenlistment bonuses are a factor in sustaining these similarities; when reenlistment rates are below target in a specialty, a bonus is added or increased. Retention profiles are also similar across the services, although differences arise from different desired force structures. For example, the Marine Corps emphasizes a junior enlisted force, whereas the Air Force seeks a more experienced enlisted force.

We view similar compensation structures and promotion systems as key mechanisms for supporting similar retention patterns within a service. Having the same compensation structure and promotion system for all personnel in a service serves to support a service's commitment to equity of opportunity, regardless of specialty. It also facilitates unit-manning practices whereby units (e.g., companies, ship crews, air wings, Marine expeditionary units) are designed to contain a particular set of specialties and yet have similar experience and rank structures regardless of specialty. Alternatively, unit-manning practices may be viewed as a response to compensation and promotion systems that largely induce similar patterns of retention and promotion among servicemembers. From this perspective, it follows that if future force structures called for manning patterns with substantially different career lengths by specialty, changes in the compensation structure and the promotion system would be necessary.

MONTHLY PAY COMPARISONS

In contrast to Tables 3.1 and 3.2, which are based on enlisted and officer personnel who served throughout all 12 months of 1999, the tables in this appendix are based on members in service in a single month, June 1999. There are two tables each for enlisted and officer personnel. The first table is based on the June 1999 pay of the members who served throughout 1999, and the second table does not impose that restriction. The second table includes members who may have arrived before or left service after June.

Table A.1

Incidence and Average Amounts of Enlisted Pay for June 1999, for Members on Active Duty All 12 Months of 1999

Type of Pay	Army		Air Force		Marine Corps		Navy	
	Pct. Rec'g	Avg. $ Amt.	Pct. Rec'g	Avg. $ Amt.	Pct. Rec'g	Avg. $ Amt.	Pct. Rec'g	Avg. $ Amt.
Basic Pay	100.0	1,624	100.0	1,695	100.0	1,466	100.0	1,642
BAH (Green Book)	100.0	537	100.0	543	100.0	516	100.0	534
BAS (Green Book)	100.0	228	100.0	228	100.0	228	100.0	228
Tax Advantage (Green Book)	100.0	143	100.0	143	100.0	136	100.0	141
Average RMC		2,533		2,609		2,345		2,545
Foreign-Duty Pay	12.7	13	10.3	13	2.9	12	2.9	14
Proficiency Pay	5.1	270	2.5	227	4.5	283	7.9	213
Overseas Extension Pay	0.2	102	0.0	62	0.9	176	0.2	172
Career Sea Pay	0.1	180	0.0		2.8	43	27.8	194
Career Sea Pay Premium	0.0	100	0.0		0.0	100	2.7	102
Hostile Fire Pay	5.4	174	7.3	206	2.9	180	9.1	189
Diving Duty Pay	0.1	179	0.2	151	0.3	183	1.6	172
Submarine Duty Pay	0.0		0.0		0.0		6.8	189
Foreign Language Pay (1)	1.2	66	1.3	77	0.5	72	0.4	70
Foreign Language Pay (2)	0.2	38	0.1	35	0.0		0.0	43
Flying Pay (Crew Member)	0.8	184	2.8	195	1.0	188	1.7	194
Flying Pay (Noncrew)	0.0		0.0		0.5	144	0.0	
Parachute Duty Pay	8.3	150	0.1	160	0.4	148	0.3	152
Flight Deck Duty Pay	0.0	150	0.0		0.4	134	2.5	142
Demolition Duty Pay	0.4	150	0.4	150	0.3	150	0.4	149

Table A.1—continued

	Army		Air Force		Marine Corps		Navy	
Type of Pay	Pct. Rec'g	Avg. $ Amt.	Pct. Rec'g	Avg. $ Amt.	Pct. Rec'g	Avg. $ Amt.	Pct. Rec'g	Avg. $ Amt.
Experiment Stress Duty	0.0	144	0.2	151	0.0	150	0.1	165
Toxic Fuels Duty Pay	0.0		0.3	150	0.0		0.0	
Toxic Pesticides Duty	0.0		0.0	79	0.0		0.0	129
High-Altitude Low Opening	0.3	227	0.3	232	0.2	225	0.5	227
Chemical Munitions Duty	0.0	149	0.0	150	0.0		0.0	150
Average S&I Pays[a]		41		31		26		116
FSA I	0.4	94	0.2	131	0.0		0.2	121
FSA II	6.9	104	3.7	135	7.1	86	6.8	102
CONUS COLA	0.4	84	0.5	36	1.0	68	0.5	78
Overseas COLA	20.3	171	19.9	258	15.1	219	15.3	256
Clothing/Uniform Allowance	8.9	275	8.8	240	11.5	221	10.0	312
Avg Misc Allowance/ COLAs[a]		67		78		65		78
Enlistment Bonus	0.6	2,176	0.1	3,734	0.0	2,083	0.3	2,069
SRB	1.1	1,649	0.9	2,546	0.0		0.4	8,152
Average Bonus[a]								
Average Monthly Pay[a]		2,641		2,718		2,437		2,739

[a]Averaged over all members, including those not receiving these pays.

Table A.2

Incidence and Average Amounts of Officer Pay for June 1999, for Members on Active Duty All 12 Months of 1999 (Commission Source Is ROTC or a Military Academy)

	Army		Air Force		Marine Corps		Navy	
Type of Pay	Pct. Rec'g	Avg. $ Amt.	Pct. Rec'g	Avg. $ Amt.	Pct. Rec'g	Avg. $ Amt.	Pct. Rec'g	Avg. $ Amt.
Basic Pay	100.0	3,784	100.0	3,792	100.0	3,590	100.0	3,668
BAH (Green Book)	100.0	866	100.0	881	100.0	869	100.0	857
BAS (Green Book)	100.0	157	100.0	157	100.0	157	100.0	157
Tax Advantage (Green Book)	100.0	313	100.0	318	100.0	296	100.0	322
Average RMC		5,121		5,148		4,913		5,004
Saved Pay	0.0		0.0		0.0		0.0	422
Health Professional Saved Pay	0.0		0.0		0.0		0.0	
Variable Special Pay	0.3	671	0.1	711	0.0		0.0	729
Board Certified Pay	1.6	298	0.9	301	0.0		0.4	336
Aviation Career Incentive Pay	9.3	488	40.2	521	31.4	464	37.7	457
Responsibility Pay	0.0		0.0		0.0		0.0	
Career Sea Pay	0.0		0.0		0.1	165	11.2	177
Career Sea Pay Premium	0.0		0.0		0.0		1.8	107
Hostile Fire Pay	5.8	176	8.7	193	4.4	165	8.3	189
Diving Duty Pay	0.0	176	0.1	157	0.3	222	2.7	191
Submarine Duty Pay	0.0		0.0		0.0		9.3	460

Table A.2—continued

Type of Pay	Army Pct. Rec'g	Army Avg. $ Amt.	Air Force Pct. Rec'g	Air Force Avg. $ Amt.	Marine Corps Pct. Rec'g	Marine Corps Avg. $ Amt.	Navy Pct. Rec'g	Navy Avg. $ Amt.
Foreign Language Pay (1)	2.7	70	2.3	86	1.1	80	0.7	77
Foreign Language Pay (2)	0.4	35	0.1	29	0.0		0.0	33
Flying Pay (Crew Member)	0.1	211	0.6	188	0.0		0.1	225
Flying Pay (Noncrew Member)	0.0	150	0.0	217	0.1	150	0.0	150
Air Weapons Controller (Crew)	0.0	156	0.8	274	0.0		0.0	200
Parachute Duty Pay	8.1	143	0.1	148	1.0	136	0.5	149
Flight Deck Duty Pay	0.0		0.0		0.1	150	1.3	136
Demolition Duty Pay	0.2	149	0.1	150	0.0	150	0.6	148
Experimental Stress Duty Pay	0.0	100	0.1	144	0.0		0.0	150
Toxic Fuels Duty Pay	0.0		0.1	142	0.0		0.0	
High-Altitude Low Opening Pay	0.1	230	0.1	230	0.0	225	0.7	225
Chemical Munitions Duty Pay	0.0	150	0.0		0.0		0.0	
Average S&I Pays[a]		77		236		156		265
FSA I	0.4	180	0.2	345	0.0		0.1	124
FSA II	4.9	106	2.8	148	6.5	89	6.2	104
CONUS COLA	0.8	126	1.5	46	1.3	113	0.9	118
Overseas COLA	18.4	306	13.0	411	10.6	457	13.0	442
Clothing/Uniform Allowance	0.1	497	0.1	554	0.0		0.2	341
Personal Money Allowance	0.0	89	0.0	42	0.0		0.0	42
Avg Misc Allowances/ COLAs[a]		64		59		56		66
Nuclear Officer Accession Bonus	0.0		0.0		0.0		0.0	2,000
Medical Officer Retention Bonus	0.1	12,987	0.0	18,058	0.0		0.0	18,000
Nuclear Career Accession Bonus	0.0		0.0		0.0		0.0	
Nuclear Career Annual Incentive Bonus	0.0		0.0		0.0		0.0	
Additional Special Pay, Medical Officer	0.0	8,857	0.1	15,000	0.0		0.0	12,833
Incentive Special Pay, Medical Officer	0.0	15,667	0.0	18,500	0.0		0.0	8,000
Nuclear-Qualified Officer Continuation	0.0		0.0		0.0		1.2	14,507
Aviation Officer Continuation	0.0		0.7	11,956	0.2	12,000	0.1	10,529
Average Bonuses[a]		22		108		24		195
Average Monthly Pay[a]		5,283		5,551		5,149		5,529

[a]Averaged over all members, including those not receiving these pays.

Table A.3

Incidence and Average Amounts of Enlisted Pay for June 1999

Type of Pay	Army		Air Force		Marine Corps		Navy	
	Pct. Rec'g	Avg. $ Amt.	Pct. Rec'g	Avg. $ Amt.	Pct. Rec'g	Avg. $ Amt.	Pct. Rec'g	Avg. $ Amt.
Basic Pay	100.0	1,551	100.0	1,647	100.0	1,401	100.0	1,562
BAH (Green Book)	100.0	528	100.0	537	100.0	508	100.0	526
BAS (Green Book)	100.0	227	100.0	228	100.0	227	100.0	227
Tax Advantage (Green Book)	100.0	140	100.0	141	100.0	133	100.0	139
Average RMC		2,447		2,553		2,269		2,454
Foreign-Duty Pay	11.3	13	9.4	13	2.4	12	2.6	13
Proficiency Pay	4.4	269	2.3	227	3.6	280	7.1	211
Overseas Extension Pay	0.2	100	0.0	62	0.7	173	0.1	175
Career Sea Pay	0.1	178	0.0		2.5	41	25.9	191
Career Sea Pay Premium	0.0	100	0.0		0.0	100	3.1	99
Hostile Fire Pay	4.7	174	6.7	206	2.4	180	8.2	188
Diving Duty Pay	0.1	178	0.2	151	0.2	181	1.4	171
Submarine Duty Pay	0.0		0.0		0.0		6.0	188
Foreign Language Pay (1)	1.2	66	1.2	77	0.4	72	0.4	70
Foreign Language Pay (2)	0.1	38	0.1	35	0.0		0.0	42
Flying Pay (Crew Member)	0.7	182	2.6	194	0.9	188	1.6	191
Flying Pay (Noncrew)	0.0		0.0		0.4	142	0.0	
Parachute Duty Pay	7.5	148	0.1	158	0.4	146	0.2	150
Flight Deck Duty Pay	0.0	150	0.0		0.3	134	2.4	143
Demolition Duty Pay	0.3	150	0.4	150	0.2	150	0.3	149
Experiment Stress Duty	0.0	144	0.2	149	0.0	146	0.1	164
Toxic Fuels Duty Pay	0.0		0.3	150	0.0		0.0	
Toxic Pesticides Duty	0.0		0.0	85	0.0		0.0	131
High-Altitude Low Opening	0.2	227	0.2	233	0.1	225	0.4	227
Chemical Munitions Duty	0.0	148	0.0	150	0.0		0.0	150
Average S&I Pays[a]		36		29		22		105
FSA I	0.4	77	0.2	118	0.0	3	0.2	96
FSA II	6.8	101	3.6	133	6.6	86	6.3	101
CONUS COLA	0.4	83	0.5	36	0.9	67	0.5	77
Overseas COLA	18.1	168	18.2	254	12.9	213	13.6	251
Clothing/Uniform Allowance	9.2	267	9.2	233	11.3	224	11.5	296
Avg Misc Allowance/ COLAs[a]		62		73		59		75
Enlistment Bonus	0.6	2,182	0.1	3,577	0.0	2,078	0.3	2,010
SRB	1.0	1,547	0.8	2,463	0.0		0.4	7,304
Average Bonus[a]		28		24		1		32
Average Monthly Pay[a]		2,546		2,654		2,350		2,634

[a]Averaged over all members, including those not receiving these pays.

Table A.4

Incidence and Average Amounts of Officer Pay for June 1999 (Commission Source Is ROTC or a Military Academy)

Type of Pay	Army Pct. Rec'g	Army Avg. $ Amt.	Air Force Pct. Rec'g	Air Force Avg. $ Amt.	Marine Corps Pct. Rec'g	Marine Corps Avg. $ Amt.	Navy Pct. Rec'g	Navy Avg. $ Amt.
Basic Pay	100.0	3,690	100.0	3,722	100.0	3,504	100.0	3,574
BAH (Green Book)	100.0	848	100.0	868	100.0	852	100.0	837
BAS (Green Book)	100.0	157	100.0	157	100.0	157	100.0	157
Tax Advantage (Green Book)	100.0	304	100.0	312	100.0	289	100.0	312
Average RMC		4,998		5,059		4,802		4,880
Saved Pay	0.0		0.0		0.0		0.0	422
Health Professional Saved Pay	0.0		0.0		0.0		0.0	
Variable Special Pay	0.3	669	0.0	711	0.0		0.0	729
Board Certified Pay	1.5	299	0.9	303	0.0		0.4	343
Aviation Career Incentive Pay	8.9	485	38.8	525	29.5	466	35.2	459
Responsibility Pay	0.0		0.0		0.0		0.0	
Career Sea Pay	0.0		0.0		0.1	165	10.5	176
Career Sea Pay Premium	0.0		0.0		0.0		1.7	108
Hostile Fire Pay	5.4	175	8.4	193	4.2	164	7.8	189
Diving Duty Pay	0.0	176	0.1	157	0.3	220	2.5	191
Submarine Duty Pay	0.0		0.0		0.0		8.8	459
Foreign Language Pay (1)	2.5	70	2.2	86	1.0	81	0.6	78
Foreign Language Pay (2)	0.3	35	0.1	30	0.0		0.0	33
Flying Pay (Crew Member)	0.1	211	0.5	188	0.0		0.1	225
Flying Pay (Noncrew Member)	0.0	150	0.0	217	0.1	150	0.0	150
Air Weapons Controller (Crew)	0.0	156	0.8	275	0.0		0.0	200
Parachute Duty Pay	7.7	143	0.1	148	0.9	137	0.4	149
Flight Deck Duty Pay	0.0		0.0		0.1	150	1.2	137
Demolition Duty Pay	0.2	149	0.0	150	0.0	150	0.6	148
Experimental Stress Duty Pay	0.0	100	0.1	144	0.0		0.0	150
Toxic Fuels Duty Pay	0.0		0.0	142	0.0		0.0	
High-Altitude Low Opening Pay	0.1	230	0.1	230	0.1	225	0.6	225
Chemical Munitions Duty Pay	0.0	150	0.0		0.0		0.0	
Average S&I Pays[a]		73		229		147		248
FSA I	0.4	178	0.2	337	0.0		0.1	84
FSA II	4.7	106	2.7	149	6.1	88	5.8	105
CONUS COLA	0.8	125	1.4	46	1.3	111	1.0	111
Overseas COLA	17.3	305	12.4	411	10.0	459	12.2	440
Clothing/Uniform Allowance	3.6	251	2.7	307	1.8	300	5.1	281
Personal Money Allowance	0.0	89	0.0	42	0.0		0.0	42
Avg Misc Allowances/ COLAs[a]		68		64		58		75

Table A.4—continued

Type of Pay	Army Pct. Rec'g	Army Avg. $ Amt.	Air Force Pct. Rec'g	Air Force Avg. $ Amt.	Marine Corps Pct. Rec'g	Marine Corps Avg. $ Amt.	Navy Pct. Rec'g	Navy Avg. $ Amt.
Nuclear Officer Accession Bonus	0.0		0.0		0.0		0.0	6,800
Medical Officer Retention Bonus	0.1	12,987	0.0	18,058	0.0		0.0	18,000
Nuclear Career Accession Bonus	0.0		0.0		0.0		0.0	
Nuclear Career Annual Incentive Bonus	0.0		0.0		0.0		0.0	
Additional Special Pay, Medical Officer	0.0	8,857	0.1	15,000	0.0		0.0	12,833
Incentive Special Pay, Medical Officer	0.0	15,667	0.0	18,500	0.0		0.0	8,000
Nuclear-Qualified Officer Continuation	0.0		0.0		0.0		1.1	14,507
Aviation Officer Continuation	0.0		0.7	11,778	0.2	12,000	0.1	10,529
Average Bonuses[a]		20		102		23		180
Average Monthly Pay[a]		5,160		5,455		5,030		5,383

[a]Averaged over all members, including those not receiving these pays.

ADDITIONAL OFFICER PAY TABLES

Table 3.2 in the body of this report is based on officers commissioned from ROTC or a military academy. Table B.1 expands that population by including officers whose source of commission was OCS, OCT, or direct appointment. In other words, Table B.1 is based on all commissioned officers. Table B.2 adds warrant officers. As in Table 3.2, Tables B.1 and B.2 are based on those who served all 12 months of 1999.

Table B.1

Incidence and Average Amounts of Officer Pay, All Commissioned Officers, 1999

Type of Pay	Army Pct. Rec'g	Army Avg. $ Amt.	Air Force Pct. Rec'g	Air Force Avg. $ Amt.	Marine Corps Pct. Rec'g	Marine Corps Avg. $ Amt.	Navy Pct. Rec'g	Navy Avg. $ Amt.
Basic Pay	100.0	3,784	100.0	3,792	100.0	3,590	100.0	3,668
BAH (Green Book)	100.0	866	100.0	881	100.0	869	100.0	857
BAS (Green Book)	100.0	157	100.0	157	100.0	157	100.0	157
Tax Advantage (Green Book)	100.0	313	100.0	318	100.0	296	100.0	322
Average RMC		5,121		5,148		4,913		5,004
Saved Pay	0.0		0.0		0.0		0.0	422
Health Professional Saved Pay	0.0		0.0		0.0		0.0	
Variable Special Pay	0.3	671	0.1	711	0.0		0.0	729
Board-Certified Pay	1.6	298	0.9	301	0.0		0.4	336
Aviation Career Incentive Pay	9.3	488	40.2	521	31.4	464	37.7	457
Responsibility Pay	0.0		0.0		0.0		0.0	
Career Sea Pay	0.0		0.0		0.1	165	11.2	177
Career Sea Pay Premium	0.0		0.0		0.0		1.8	107
Hostile Fire Pay	5.8	176	8.7	193	4.4	165	8.3	189
Diving Duty Pay	0.0	176	0.1	157	0.3	222	2.7	191
Submarine Duty Pay	0.0		0.0		0.0		9.3	460
Foreign Language Pay (1)	2.7	70	2.3	86	1.1	80	0.7	77
Foreign Language Pay (2)	0.4	35	0.1	29	0.0		0.0	33
Flying Pay (Crew Member)	0.1	211	0.6	188	0.0		0.1	225
Flying Pay (Noncrew Member)	0.0	150	0.0	217	0.1	150	0.0	150
Air Weapons Controller (Crew)	0.0	156	0.8	274	0.0		0.0	200

Table B.1—continued

Type of Pay	Army		Air Force		Marine Corps		Navy	
	Pct. Rec'g	Avg. $ Amt.	Pct. Rec'g	Avg. $ Amt.	Pct. Rec'g	Avg. $ Amt.	Pct. Rec'g	Avg. $ Amt.
Parachute Duty Pay	8.1	143	0.1	148	1.0	136	0.5	149
Flight Deck Duty Pay	0.0		0.0		0.1	150	1.3	136
Demolition Duty Pay	0.2	149	0.1	150	0.0	150	0.6	148
Experimental Stress Duty Pay	0.0	100	0.1	144	0.0		0.0	150
Toxic Fuels Duty Pay	0.0		0.1	142	0.0		0.0	
High-Altitude Low Opening Pay	0.1	230	0.1	230	0.0	225	0.7	225
Chemical Munitions Duty Pay	0.0	150	0.0		0.0		0.0	
Average S&I Pays[a]		77		236		156		265
FSA I	0.4	180	0.2	345	0.0		0.1	124
FSA II	4.9	106	2.8	148	6.5	89	6.2	104
CONUS COLA	0.8	126	1.5	46	1.3	113	0.9	118
Overseas COLA	18.4	306	13.0	411	10.6	457	13.0	442
Clothing/Uniform Allowance	0.1	497	0.1	554	0.0		0.2	341
Personal Money Allowance	0.0	89	0.0	42	0.0		0.0	42
Avg Misc Allowance/ COLAs[a]		64		59		56		66
Nuclear Officer Accession Bonus	0.0		0.0		0.0		0.0	2,000
Medical Officer Retention Bonus	0.1	12,987	0.0	18,058	0.0		0.0	18,000
Nuclear Career Accession Bonus	0.0		0.0		0.0		0.0	
Nuclear Career Annual Incentive Bonus	0.0		0.0		0.0		0.0	
Additional Special Pay, Medical Officer	0.0	8,857	0.1	15,000	0.0		0.0	12,833
Incentive Special Pay, Medical Officer	0.0	15,667	0.0	18,500	0.0		0.0	8,000
Nuclear-Qualified Officer Continuation	0.0		0.0		0.0		1.2	14,507
Aviation Officer Continuation	0.0		0.7	11,956	0.2	12,000	0.1	10,529
Average Bonus[a]		22		108		24		195
Average Monthly Pay[a]		5,283		5,551		5,149		5,529

[a]Averaged over all members, including those not receiving these pays.

Table B.2

Incidence and Average Amounts of Officer Pay, All Commissioned Officers and Warrant Officers, 1999

Type of Pay	Army		Air Force		Marine Corps		Navy	
	Pct. Rec'g	Avg. $ Amt.	Pct. Rec'g	Avg. $ Amt.	Pct. Rec'g	Avg. $ Amt.	Pct. Rec'g	Avg. $ Amt.
Basic Pay	100.0	3,690	100.0	3,722	100.0	3,504	100.0	3,574
BAH (Green Book)	100.0	848	100.0	868	100.0	852	100.0	837
BAS (Green Book)	100.0	157	100.0	157	100.0	157	100.0	157

Table B.2—continued

Type of Pay	Army Pct. Rec'g	Army Avg. $ Amt.	Air Force Pct. Rec'g	Air Force Avg. $ Amt.	Marine Corps Pct. Rec'g	Marine Corps Avg. $ Amt.	Navy Pct. Rec'g	Navy Avg. $ Amt.
Tax Advantage (Green Book)	100.0	304	100.0	312	100.0	289	100.0	312
Average RMC		4,998		5,059		4,802		4,880
Saved Pay	0.0		0.0		0.0		0.0	422
Health Professional Saved Pay	0.0		0.0		0.0		0.0	
Variable Special Pay	0.3	669	0.0	711	0.0		0.0	729
Board-Certified Pay	1.5	299	0.9	303	0.0		0.4	343
Aviation Career Incentive Pay	8.9	485	38.8	525	29.5	466	35.2	459
Responsibility Pay	0.0		0.0		0.0		0.0	
Career Sea Pay	0.0		0.0		0.1	165	10.5	176
Career Sea Pay Premium	0.0		0.0		0.0		1.7	108
Hostile Fire Pay	5.4	175	8.4	193	4.2	164	7.8	189
Diving Duty Pay	0.0	176	0.1	157	0.3	220	2.5	191
Submarine Duty Pay	0.0		0.0		0.0		8.8	459
Foreign Language Pay (1)	2.5	70	2.2	86	1.0	81	0.6	78
Foreign Language Pay (2)	0.3	35	0.1	30	0.0		0.0	33
Flying Pay (Crew Member)	0.1	211	0.5	188	0.0		0.1	225
Flying Pay (Noncrew Member)	0.0	150	0.0	217	0.1	150	0.0	150
Air Weapons Controller (Crew)	0.0	156	0.8	275	0.0		0.0	200
Parachute Duty Pay	7.7	143	0.1	148	0.9	137	0.4	149
Flight Deck Duty Pay	0.0		0.0		0.1	150	1.2	137
Demolition Duty Pay	0.2	149	0.0	150	0.0	150	0.6	148
Experimental Stress Duty Pay	0.0	100	0.1	144	0.0		0.0	150
Toxic Fuels Duty Pay	0.0		0.0	142	0.0		0.0	
High-Altitude Low Opening Pay	0.1	230	0.1	230	0.1	225	0.6	225
Chemical Munitions Duty Pay	0.0	150	0.0		0.0		0.0	
Average S&I Pays[a]		73		229		147		248
FSA I	0.4	178	0.2	337	0.0		0.1	84
FSA II	4.7	106	2.7	149	6.1	88	5.8	105
CONUS COLA	0.8	125	1.4	46	1.3	111	1.0	111
Overseas COLA	17.3	305	12.4	411	10.0	459	12.2	440
Clothing/Uniform Allowance	3.6	251	2.7	307	1.8	300	5.1	281
Personal Money Allowance	0.0	89	0.0	42	0.0		0.0	42
Avg Misc Allowance/ COLAs[a]		68		64		58		75
Nuclear Officer Accession Bonus	0.0		0.0		0.0		0.0	6,800
Medical Officer Retention Bonus	0.1	12,987	0.0	18,058	0.0		0.0	18,000
Nuclear Career Accession Bonus	0.0		0.0		0.0		0.0	

Table B.2—continued

Type of Pay	Army		Air Force		Marine Corps		Navy	
	Pct. Rec'g	Avg. $ Amt.	Pct. Rec'g	Avg. $ Amt.	Pct. Rec'g	Avg. $ Amt.	Pct. Rec'g	Avg. $ Amt.
Nuclear Career Annual Incentive Bonus	0.0		0.0		0.0		0.0	
Additional Special Pay, Medical Officer	0.0	8,857	0.1	15,000	0.0		0.0	12,833
Incentive Special Pay, Medical Officer	0.0	15,667	0.0	18,500	0.0		0.0	8,000
Nuclear-Qualified Officer Continuation	0.0		0.0		0.0		1.1	14,507
Aviation Officer Continuation	0.0		0.7	11,778	0.2	12,000	0.1	10,529
Average Bonus[a]		20		102		23		180
Average Monthly Pay[a]		5,160		5,455		5,030		5,383

[a]Averaged over all members, including those not receiving these pays.

BIBLIOGRAPHY

2001 Uniformed Services Almanac, Falls Church, Va.: Uniformed Services Almanac, Inc., 2001.

Kilburn, M. Rebecca, Rachel Louie, Dana P. Goldman, *Patterns of Enlisted Compensation*, Santa Monica, Calif.: RAND, MR-807-OSD, 2001.

Williamson, Stephanie, *A Description of U.S. Enlisted Personnel Promotion Systems*, Santa Monica, Calif.: RAND, MR-1067-OSD, 1999.